Images of
Preston

Images of Preston

Lancashire Evening Post

Breedon Books
Publishing Company
Derby

First published in Great Britain by
The Breedon Books Publishing Company Limited
44 Friar Gate, Derby, DE1 1DA.
1995

ISBN 1 85983 007 2

Printed and bound by Butler & Tanner, Frome, Somerset.
Cover printed by Premier Print, Nottingham.

Contents

Foreword

Preston is one of the most important towns of Northern England and the photographs in this book provide reminders from earlier times of many aspects of life in this proud and historic town.

As a Prestonian the photographs remind me of the sights and sounds of my upbringing in the town and I am sure they will provide equally vivid memories for every Prestonian.

The book offers significant insights into the development of Preston as an important centre for industry and commerce, from the Industrial Revolution to more modem times.

Preston has fine civic buildings and many of historic interest, which are celebrated in the photographs.

The people of Preston are proud and warm-hearted and support each other through difficult times. The photographs illustrate these characteristics and show aspects of the hardship which the proud people of Preston have had to bear.

The achievements of earlier generations and the rich and varied history of the town have not always been celebrated as they deserve and this book is a marvellous way of bringing the past alive for the current generation.

I am sure there is something of interest for everyone and I hope you enjoy looking at the photographs and reflecting on the achievements of Proud Preston.

Brian G. Booth
Vice-Chancellor
University of Central Lancashire
June 1995

Introduction

PRESTON can be proud of its claim to being one of the oldest boroughs in Britain. It can be proud, too, that historical records can trace its links with the Roman occupation of Britain and with succeeding Anglo-Saxon and Danish periods. There is little doubt that Preston's origin as a settlement was influenced by its situation on high ground overlooking the River Ribble.

It is believed the town got its name from Preosta-tun, meaning Priest-town, which is contained in a charter of Edward the Confessor's reign. Preston is mentioned in the Domesday Book of William the Conqueror and the first known religious foundation was at Tulketh where the Benedictine monks arrived in 1123. After a four-year stay they moved on to build Furness Abbey, and in 1221 the Franciscan friars arrived to give Friargate its name.

By then Preston had developed into a small but busy market town and in 1179 it had received a charter from Henry II permitting certain trading rights to the burgesses, or residents. This was known as a Guild Charter which is joyously celebrated every 20 years.

Preston has been the scene of several bloody battles – including the Scottish invasion in 1323 when Robert Bruce's soldiers set fire to the town, the Civil War in the time of Cromwell and the Jacobite Rebellions of 1715 and 1745.

Up to the Industrial Revolution, which began in the eighteenth century, the shape and size of Preston had remained virtually unchanged for hundreds of years. But with the coming of the Steam Age and the discovery of the Lancashire coalfields the face of the town began to alter rapidly.

As the population grew the patchwork of fields surrounding what was then only a market town began to be replaced by rows of terraced back-to-back houses, cobbled streets and forbidding factories.

The first water-powered cotton mill in Preston opened in 1777 in Moor Lane. In 1800, with the arrival of steam power in the town, there were 16 spinning mills operating.

By now more rural workers were abandoning the cottage crafts of handloom weaving and spinning to live and work in Preston. This resulted in many of them living in overcrowded houses and cellars within the shadow of the mills. In 1883 there were around 80 mills.

The cotton industry reached its peak around 1914, but after World War One it began to decline because of overseas competition. The last cotton mill to be built in Preston was the Embroidery Mill in 1913.

After World War Two, Preston adapted to a diversity of industries – the main one being aircraft production which was later transferred to neighbouring Warton and Samlesbury.

Great development schemes were also undertaken after the war in Preston and many areas in the town were demolished and replaced with modern buildings and new roads.

The many photographs in this book provide a visual record of some of Preston's former places, characters and past events which are sure to interest readers of all ages.

Something sensational must have happened here! This was the usual scene on Preston Market Square when General Election results were announced in the days before radio sets had become popular. The results were flashed on to the large screen from a projector on the old Town Hall steps after midnight. This photograph was taken in 1931 from the Harris Library.

This 1959 presentation by Hutton and Howick Women's Institute recaptured the spirit of the Roaring Twenties when they showed off the styles of the Flapper era.

WHY YOU SHOULD VOTE
FOR

FLORENCE WHITE

The Policy of the Government is Fixed, therefore, A Vote for Either Party is Wasted.

BRITAIN EXPECTS –

BRITAIN EXPECTS –

THE ONLY ISSUE AT THIS ELECTION IS WHETHER SPINSTERS SHALL OR SHALL NOT HAVE JUSTICE

CITIZENS OF PRESTON IT RESTS WITH YOU!

A pension for spinsters! That was the clarion call by Miss Florence White in her lone battle to win the 1936 Preston parliamentary by-election. She polled only 3,221 votes out of the 66,000 cast. The winner was the Conservative candidate Capt E.C.Cobb.

These halberds alongside the entrance of this house always marked the home of the current Mayor of Preston. The home in the picture was that of Alderman Dr Derham, of Garstang Road, Preston. He was mayor of the town in 1933.

Preston Fire Brigade, 1935, in their gleaming brass Roman-style helmets and jackboots outside their fire station, then in Tithebarn Street. They were an impressive sight whenever they took part in the mayoral processions. This fire station was built in 1852 and demolished around 1967 to make way for the new bus station.

Ladies had their own tables for many years in the Harris Library's General Reading Room which had many varied newspapers and periodicals. This was converted to offices in the late 1960s and a much smaller reading section was allocated to the lending department.

Behind the scenes at the Harris Lending Library. All female librarians had to wear dark blue overalls with a white collar when on duty. This was relaxed after World War Two.

The Harris Library used to have a directories counter in addition to its book lending service. This picture was taken in 1935.

The Children's Library within the Harris building was a huge success when it first opened in 1935.

The Harris Reference Library in 1936. It has had some changes since then, but the craftsman-made furniture still remains in use.

IRA activities were causing problems in the North-West as far back as 1939 when this picture was taken. A Preston Harris Library official is seen checking shopping baskets and parcels being carried into the building. The scare then was only short-lived.

The Three Graces – but not the costly ones recently in danger of being sold to the USA. This trio of virgins are seen here in the Harris building soon after the unveiling in 1926 of the war memorial names on the stairway.

Women cleaners were usually known as charwomen up to around World War Two. These two ladies in dustcaps and aprons are sprucing up Niobe and her young daughter at the Harris Art Gallery in 1935.

The corporation's Argyll Road refuse destructor in 1886 soon after it was built.

The only protective clothing this corporation dustman had in 1934 was an old sack for an apron.

Animal fat used to be collected from the slaughter-houses and butchers to be extracted in these vats at the Corporation Destructors in Argyll Road, Deepdale.

Men at work in 1940. This incinerator was installed when the Corporation Destructor Works, Argyll Road, was opened in 1886. The refuse was shovel-fed by gangs of men on to a grid and conveyed to furnaces. Nowadays the refuse is taken by lorry to Freckleton Marsh tip.

Not much has changed here except in name. The new Municipal Building being completed. The tramlines in Lancaster Road are visible.

Preston's Municipal Building was officially opened on 14 September 1933. That night it was bathed in floodlights (to the right) and crowds danced to a band on the Market Square. In 1972 the council changed its name to the Town Hall.

Schoolchildren in relays were shown round the new Municipal Building (now the Town Hall) when it first opened in 1933. Here they are being shown the mayoral chair in the council chamber.

The bull-ring stone on Preston Market Square dates back centuries. The bull was tethered to a ring and dogs set upon the animal. The practice was stopped by the corporation around 1726 because too many fights broke out around it over the wild noisy betting. The stone is still there.

The old Town Hall as it looked soon after it was built in 1862. The cloisters are on the Fishergate side.

The lovely inside entrance to the old Town Hall which was destroyed by fire. The five sculptures were saved and are now in the Harris Museum.

Firemen on a turntable ladder pouring water into the old Town Hall clock tower at the height of the blaze on, 15 March 1947. Its loss was felt by everyone in the area.

Part of the old Town Hall was renovated for a time with limited use. It was finally demolished in 1962 and replaced by Crystal House block of shops and offices.

This picture taken on Cheapside after the Town Hall fire shows the massive clock bells which fell down inside the clock tower, sounding the building's death knell. The bells were the largest in England outside Westminster.

Down it falls. The pinnacle of the old Town Hall faceless clock tower being demolished after the fire.

This building, the Preston Gas Company office and showroom in Fishergate, was demolished in 1964 to make way for the St George's Shopping Centre entrance opposite Woolworths. It was built in 1877 and then owned by a private company. It was nationalised after World War Two.

This tunnel beneath Longridge Fell was bored around 1930 to convey water from the reservoirs to Preston.

Fulwood Barracks as it looked around World War One. The barracks were built in 1847 and revamped around 1964 when the archway was removed. The royal crest, on top, now stands on the barracks front lawn.

The old Unitarian chapel, set back off Church Street, was a religious meeting house in 1716 and is one of Preston's oldest buildings. It was the town's first dissenting chapel; graves lie beneath the shrubbery.

Saul Street Methodist chapel was opened in 1837. It was bought later by the Freemasons and opened as a Masonic Temple in 1944 after which it was refronted and additions made.

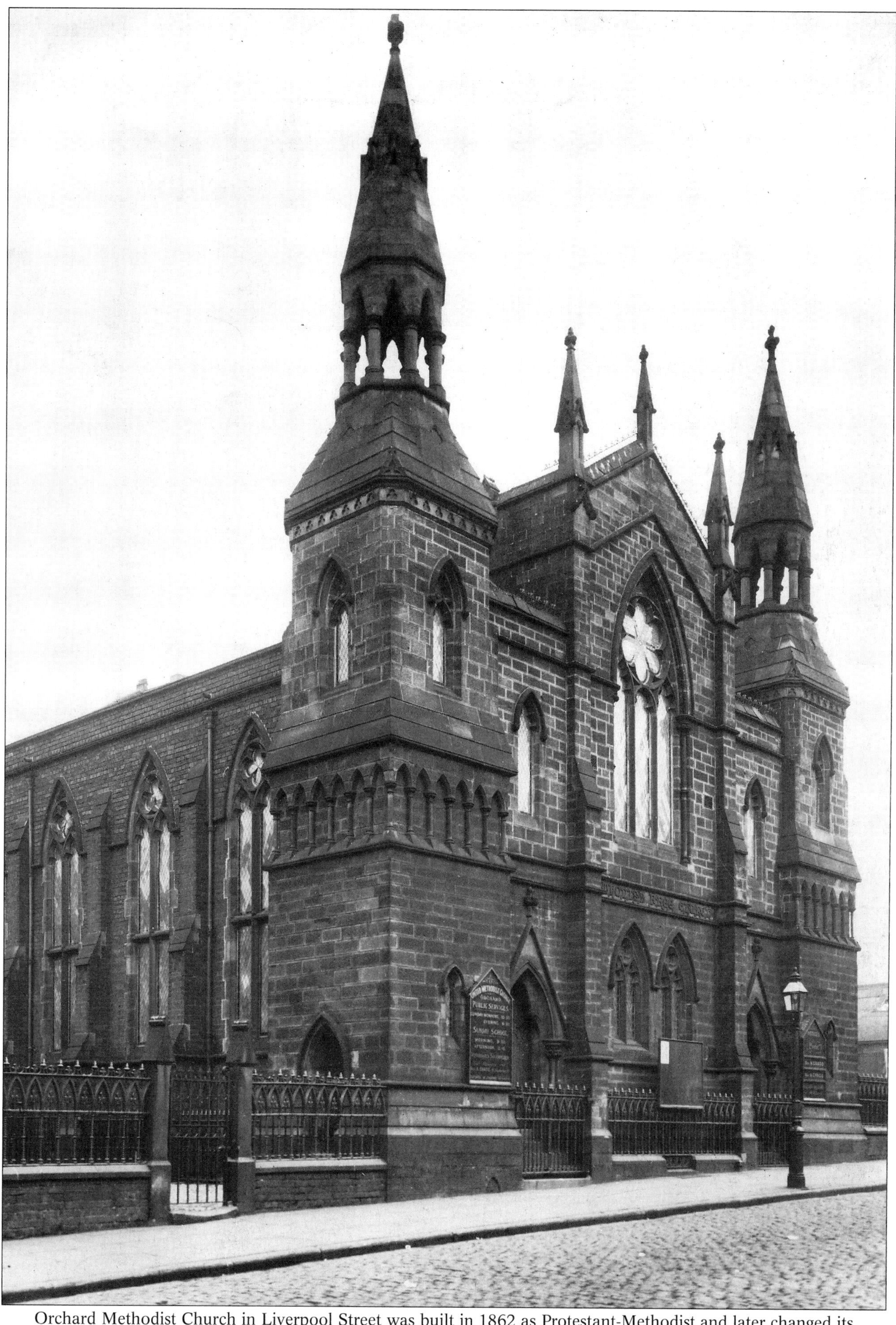

Orchard Methodist Church in Liverpool Street was built in 1862 as Protestant-Methodist and later changed its affiliation to Wesleyan, and then to United Methodist in 1932. The chapel was built on what was Chadwick's Orchard. It closed in 1954 and later the site became part of the Market Hall.

Holy Trinity Church off Market Street was demolished in 1951 and the parish merged with St George's. The former graveyard is now used as a car-park.

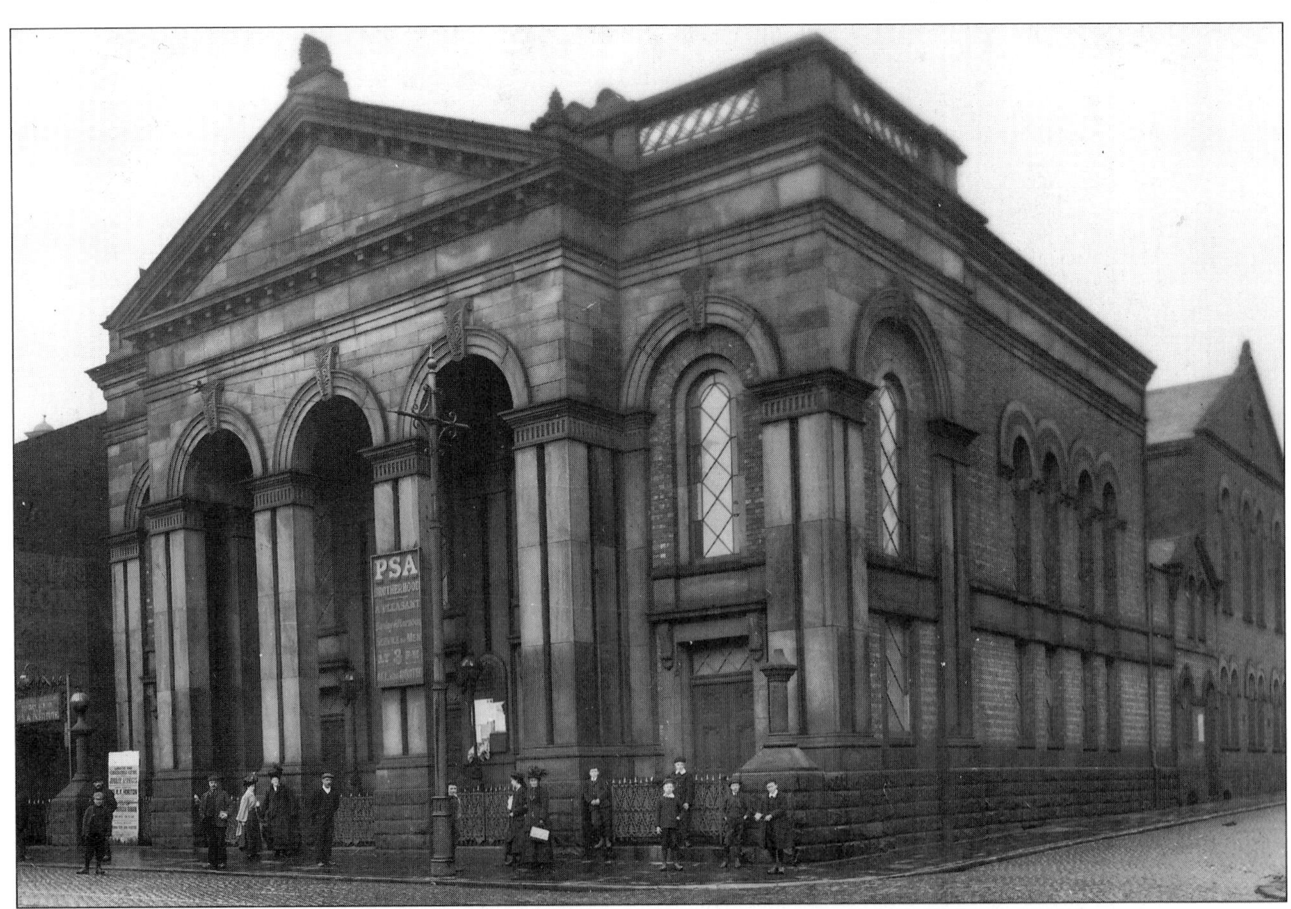

Lancaster Road Congregational Church, built in 1863, is now the site of Duchy House office block. The church was built by worshippers who had broken away from Cannon Street Congregationalists. The notice board says, 'PSA', which stood for Pleasant Sunday Afternoon services. In 1954 the pillared entrance was changed.

St Saviour's Church, formerly in Leeming Street, was built in 1868 and was within a short distance of the old St James' Church with which it merged in 1970 and then closed down.

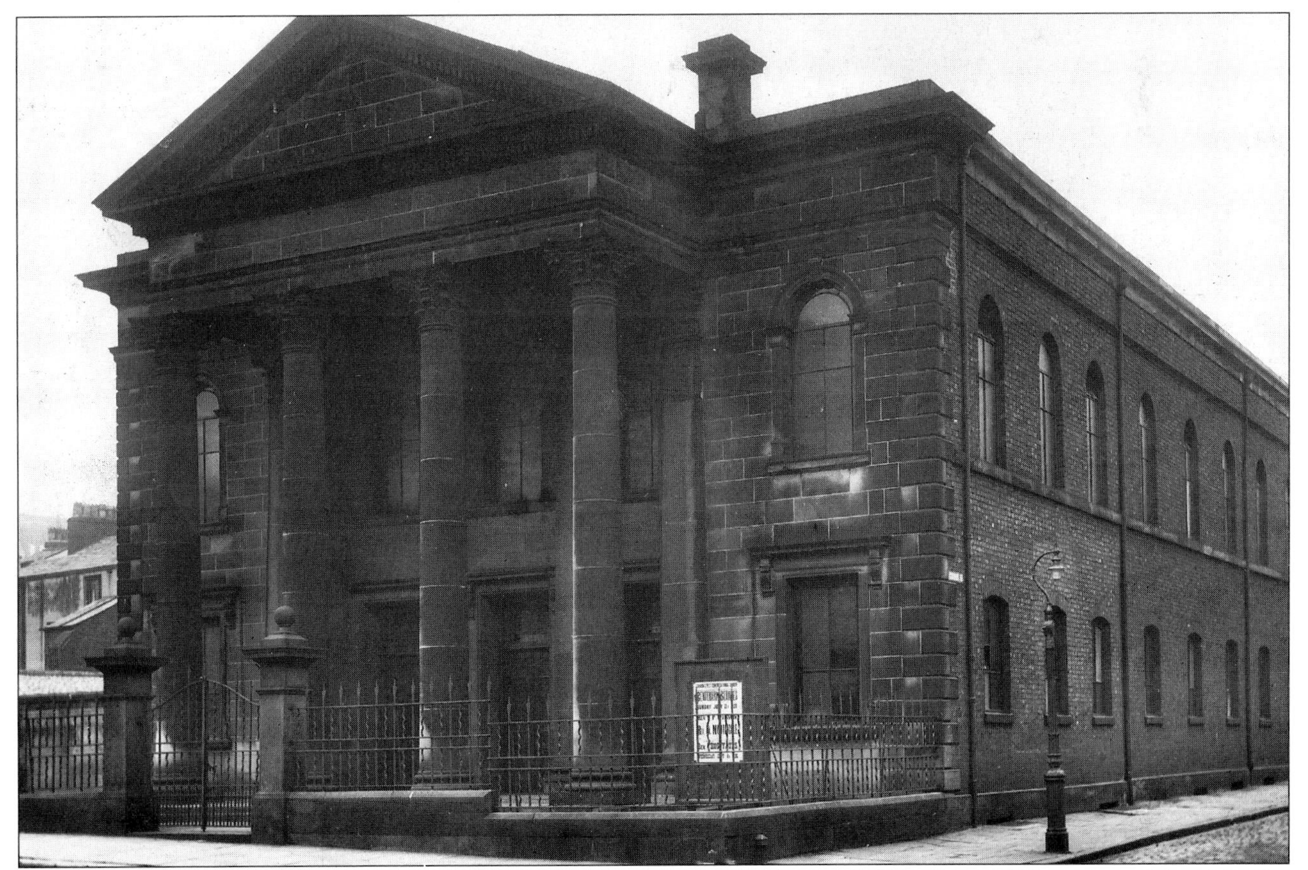

Opened in 1826, Cannon Street Congregational Church stood at the corner of that street and Cross Street. In 1852 the entrance was moved to the other end of the church (as seen here) in Guildhall Street. Offices are now on this site.

This building, which is still in Cannon Street, was used from 1828 as the Institution for the Diffusion of Useful Knowledge. It ceased as such in 1849 when the Harris Institute, Avenham, was opened.

Not many Catholic churches have vanished from the local scene. But this one, St Mary's, which stood in a quiet yard off Friargate was swept away in 1993.

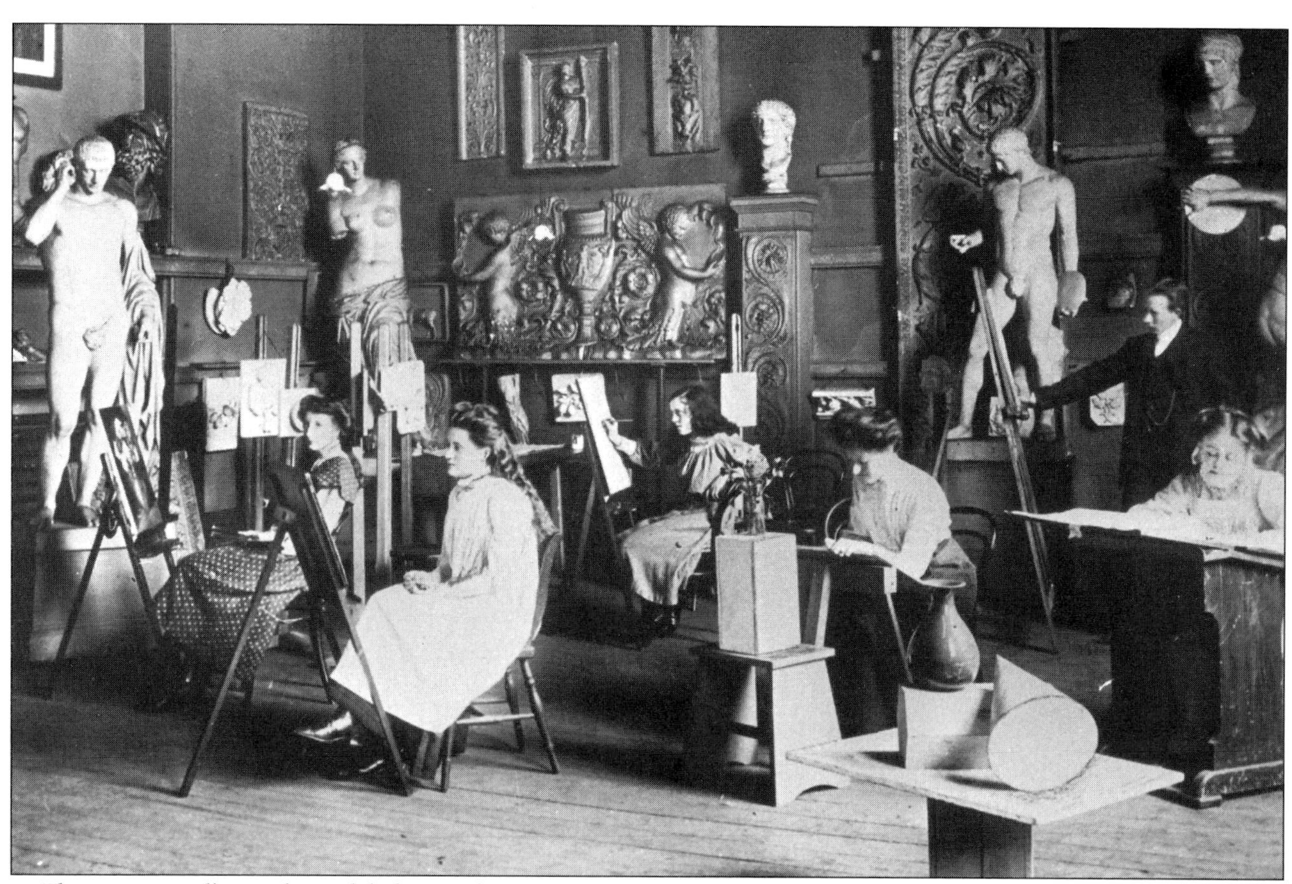

There were no live nude models for art classes – just fig-leaved statues – when this photo was taken at the Harris Avenham Institute in 1914.

This lovely old building was demolished in 1956 during a wave of demolitions involving several graceful properties in the Winckley Square area. It is the old Preston Grammar School, built in 1841 in Cross Street at the corner of Guildhall Street. Increasing numbers of pupils necessitated the building of the new Grammar School in Moor Park Avenue in 1913.

School days were clearly happy days at the former Preston Grammar School in 1934 when this was taken. The school in Moor Park Avenue is now Parklands High.

Prefects of Preston Grammar School pose by the stonework entrance, in 1932, which had just been transferred from the old school in Cross Street.

Nuclear physics would hardly be known to these keen young science students at Preston Grammar School in 1932.

These 1939 gym-slip students in the commercial department of the Harris Technical College are under the watchful eye of department head Mr G.Webster (left) with the winged-collar. The boys are segregated at the back of the class. The college is now part of Central Lancashire University, Corporation Street.

This scene in Garstang Road shows English Martyrs' Infants and Girls' Schools were both becoming structurally unsafe in 1973 when brickwork of an adjoining shop crashed into the girls' empty playground. A new primary school was built nearby in Sizer Street soon afterwards and Canterbury Hall erected on the old school site.

Echoes of the Past

In 1850 Preston Market Square looked like this. The Harris Library building was erected on the site where the shops were.

The historic obelisk, erected in 1782 on the Market Square, is seen on this rare photograph taken before 1853 when it was removed by the corporation. It was restored to the square in 1979 to commemorate Preston's octocentenary and unveiled by the Queen.

The old Starch houses around 1900 in what was Starchhouse Square which have long since gone. The Covered Market can be seen in the distant right. The square vanished around 1965.

Tithebarn Street had thatched cottages here in 1904 – with the old cotton mill (fronting Lord Street) in the background

Historic Arkwright House, in Stoneygate, where Sir Richard Arkwright made his spinning frame in 1732, looked like this in the 1930s. From a select wealthy residence it had descended into a disreputable beerhouse and then into a common lodging house. It was saved from demolition by a heritage group and reopened as an educational centre by Princess Alexandra in 1980. It is now used by Age Concern.

Cragg's Row has changed since this scene around 1895, but the old windmill is still there. In the distance is the Ebenezer Chapel which later became Bennets' Electric Theatre one of the town's first silent-film cinemas. On the right is Singleton Row.

Miller Arcade, built in 1901, was Preston's first élite shopping precinct. In addition to Hayhurst's Kings Arms on the corner it also had a Turkish Baths and the Geisha Dance Hall. The arcade was owned by local dentist Nathaniel Miller.

The Sir Robert Peel limestone statue in Winckley Square is still there, but the name of the Mayor of Preston who unveiled it in 1852 has been erased from the plinth (see arrow). He was Dr Thomas Monk, 61, who was jailed for life in 1857 for a minor forgery offence. Afterwards the corporation obliterated his name.

This view from the top of Cannon Street shows the Grey Horse and Seven Stars which fronted Fishergate. Soon after this picture was taken in 1920 it was turned into shops. The rear part of the inn was bought by George Toulmin to join part of the *Lancashire Evening Post.*

This shows the Grey Horse and Seven Stars from a different aspect in 1923 when it was closed down after being bought by George Toulmin's sons to extend the *Lancashire Evening Post's* premises in Fishergate. The Borough Tavern was also bought by the Toulmin family for extensions to the press-room.

St John's Place which links Church Street, alongside Preston Parish Church, down to Stoneygate was widened in 1937 and the old cottages demolished.

Handloom weavers occupied these cellared cottages once in Mount Pleasant, off Corporation Street.

Everton Gardens, off North Road, had more cobblestones than flowers. Here's how it looked in 1939. It was cleared away in the 1960s to make way for the new bus station.

This is reputed to be the oldest shop in Preston. Situated in Market Place (opposite the Flag Market) it was a tobacconists for many years until about 1964. It still remains, but not as a tobacconists.

Clark's Yard – a thoroughfare which was on the Town Map in 1684. This photograph was taken in 1970 shortly before it was widened to make the present service road from Church Street (seen at the end) to the Guild Hall.

The old mounting steps that once were in Black Horse Yard now called Lowthian Street. This narrow alleyway survived demolition, but the buildings on the left now form the side of the C & A store. At the top is the Market public house.

This was known as the House that Jack Built. It stood in Fylde Street on the site of Caspar House. It was reputed to have been built in a day for a wager in 1869.

Ribbleton Hall, formerly near Ribbleton Hall Drive, was demolished in 1949. It was built by wealthy lawyer Thomas Birchall who secretly and cruelly deprived his wife of her fortune and left it to his illegitimate offsprings.

The Rose Bud, trams, tram-lines and the gents' iron urinal have long been swept away at the junction of Newhall Lane, Stanley Street and London Road. There were several iron urinals in Preston until the late 1950s – nicknamed the Iron Dukes.

Traffic was getting busier in 1936, so one of the first roundabouts was built opposite the cemetery gates in Newhall Lane. The keepers' lodges remained until around 1950.

The policeman on point-duty at Withy Trees corner, Fulwood, had a quiet time in 1930 when this picture was taken from the Methodist Church side. The petrol station on the left has been rebuilt twice since this was taken.

Where sheep may safely graze – at least at one time! This view is of Lytham Road, Fulwood, around 1925 and was taken looking west from the railway tunnel. The corner of Inkerman Street is visible on the left and houses now cover the rest.

Straight ahead is the start of Blackpool Road from what is now Newhall Lane roundabout. Point duty borough policemen were more conspicuous in their white coats. On the right is the cemetery keeper's lodge which was demolished after World War Two.

Recognise this corner? It is Blackpool Road (looking towards Deepdale). On the left and right is Ribbleton Avenue which cuts across. On the front right is Willow Crescent and the year is 1932.

Cyclists were safer passing the junction of Blackpool Road and Deepdale Road in 1932. On the far left corner the Deepdale disabled unit is now sited.

Penwortham Bridge at the bottom of Fishergate Hill is seen being constructed in 1916. Allsop's shipyard is seen on the right.

Who would think that this was Liverpool Road, Penwortham. Ahead is the hill, on the left Leyland Road triangle. The date, 1932.

Penwortham's Liverpool Road was still a quiet thoroughfare in 1951 when this was taken. The view is towards Preston and the Fleece Inn is at the end of the row of cottages on the right.

If only Longton village could have remained as peaceful and traffic-free as it once was in 1939 when the *Post* photographer took this picture. Straight ahead is the Golden Ball.

Resurfacing Blackpool Road, Ashton, with tar macadam in 1935, soon after the last tram service ended. The tram lines can be seen and the overhead power lines have been converted to lighting standards on one side of the road. This section of Blackpool Road between Inkerman Street and Lively Polly Corner (at the far end) was then called Long Lane.

The fruit and fish merchant on his rounds with his horse and cart opposite the Tardy Gate Inn, Lostock Hall around 1914.

Blackpool Road, looking west, from a point near Moor Park Serpentine. This road was only a lane until 1925 when it was widened as a circular road for Blackpool-bound traffic. It was first called the New Arterial Road.

Concreting Preston's roads and streets found work for many unemployed men during the 'Hungry Thirties'. The scene is Blackpool Road almost opposite what is now Do It All.

St Vincent's Boys' Home, in Fulwood, opened in 1896, was run by the Sisters of Charity for destitute children. It was demolished in 1956 and the youngsters boarded in ordinary homes. Afterwards St Thomas More High School was built on the site and later renamed Corpus Christi High School.

The first group of children to be placed in the care of St Vincent's Home in 1896. The sisters' dress was similar to the French peasants in the area from which they were founded.

St Vincent's Boys' Band around 1920. It was renowned in the Preston area until the home closed down in 1956. The home accommodated around 300 boys.

Black Bull Lane, Fulwood, in 1937 presents a peaceful setting. This picture was taken from Queen's Drive looking south. The entrance to Fulwood Leisure Centre is now on the right, where the double telegraph poles stand. (*Photo: Harris Library*)

The same Black Bull Lane bend, looking north. This view is from the entrance to a narrow lane which led to Scott's Farm and is now Conway Drive (left). Corporation buses at that time terminated at Boys Lane. (*Photo: Harris Library*)

This was Fylde Street in 1937 (looking east). It is the site of a busy double roundabout where Fylde Road, Adelphi Street, Moor Lane, Walker Street, Friargate and Corporation Street all join. On the left now is Caspar House office block. (*Photo: Harris Library*)

This scene, too, is now part of the same roundabout. The photograph was taken from Kendal Street which now leads to the main front entrance, off Corporation Street, to Central Lancashire University. The peaked-roof building in the distance was the gas-works – now Telephone House. (*Photo: Harris Library*)

Lune Street, where it joined Friargate, in 1939. Wildings decorators is first on the left, then Preston Farmers Trading. On the corner is Pegrams grocers. In Friargate Sterlings shoes and Harrops furniture can be seen. This is now part of Ringway.

The Little John Inn (on the nearest left corner) and all the houses in Atkinson Street were awaiting clearance in 1959 when this picture was taken. At the far end is Lancaster Road.

Mill Hill Street, where Fylde Road (left) and Fylde Street (right) meet was the site of one of Preston's three former windmills. The properties on their right are now gone. At the top of Mill Hill can be seen Mill Hill Ragged School.

This ghostly looking tunnel runs beneath a part of Preston and was once a busy rail link between Preston Station and the old Longridge Station. Opened in 1847 it burrows under Fylde Road in three lengths, emerging completely at St Paul's Road. The rail service now ends at Deepdale coal sidings and only two weekday trains travel along the route.

Many people wonder how Aqueduct Street got its name. Here is the answer. This narrow bridge carried the Lancaster Canal, until 1964, when this section of the canal was drained, the bridge demolished and the street widened up to Fylde Road. Shelley Mill is visible (left) in the distance. *(picture: Vanished Preston, Harris Museum)*

Adelphi Street was once a busy street lined with small shops. These stood opposite Hawkins' Mill lodge wall until the area was cleared in 1965 during a wave of demolitions in the town, many of which were later regretted.

Park Road is now part of Ringway, near St Paul's Square. On the right Pole Street can just be seen.

Arch Street was in the shadow of Horrocks's factory. Attempts to preserve the street as a piece of industrial history failed.

At one time Preston's greatest public benefactor Edmund Harris lived here at Whinfield Mansion, Whinfield Lane, Ashton. The front of the house overlooked Ashton Park and the rear Ashton Marsh and the Ribble.

Pedder's Lane where it joined Watery Lane, Ashton, in 1933. The mansion behind the Shell-Mex lorry was the home of the Galloway cotton magnate family and was called The Willows. The Galloways bequeathed the mansion to the town as a convalescent home. The junction is now a busy wide link to Riversway.

The wholesale fruit and vegetable warehouses which used to line Liverpool Street. The Market Hall is now in its place. The wholesale market was moved to Bow Lane around 1965.

The Corporation Arms and other buildings at the bottom of Lune Street were cleared in 1965 to make way for Ringway. The Corporation Arms belonged to the corporation in earlier times and was pock-marked by grapeshot in the 1842 cotton riots. The flowerbed (left) is in front of the Corn Exchange.

Scout Motors garage and offices in Starchhouse Square were swept away in 1965 to make way for the new Market Hall and Ringway. The Market Tavern (on the left) still remains. In the 1930s, and later, other smaller bus firms operated from the square including Viking, BBMS, Dallas, Brookhouse Motors and Premier.

The old Apollo Inn, formerly at the corner of North Road and Walker Street. Saul Street Baths (near right) was cleared to make way for the new Crown Courts

Park Road (ahead) in 1964 has now gone. Here is where it joined Meadow Street (left), to the right was North Road corner (just off the photo). All this was cleared for Ringway.

When it first opened in 1938, the Ritz Cinema in Church Street was hailed as Preston's new super modern picture house, The first film it showed was George Formby in *Keep Fit* and the one which drew the biggest audiences was *Reach for the Sky*, when 25,725 people saw it during its two-week run. The cinema ended as a bingo house.

This caused a stir in 1950 when a driverless wagon ran backwards in London Road. No one was injured and the lamppost saved the shops, including the Troy Laundry agency next to the newsagents – all these small shops are now gone.

Gooby's will still be remembered as one of Preston's leading haberdashers in Church Street at the corner of Tithebarn Street. Their shop assistants, like many other stores, had to wear black dresses when serving. Meesons was known as a cut-price sweet shop and, at the extreme right, the Palladium Cinema can just be seen here in 1950.

What is now St George's Shopping Precinct used to be a maze of alleyways between Friargate and Fishergate. The chimney being dismantled was in narrow Aspinall Street, off Bambers Yard, which had several small shops.

There were once canal warehouses off Corporation Street close to the basin where the Preston end of the canal started.

The Star Cinema at the corner of Fylde Road and Corporation Street was a round-shaped building opened in 1926. It closed in 1960 and the site is now part of the university car-park.

The Princes Theatre, Tithebarn Street, was first known as the Gaiety. It was later owned by Will Onda who turned it into a cinema. It closed around 1960.

The Royal Hippodrome in Friargate being demolished in 1959 to make way for C & A's store.

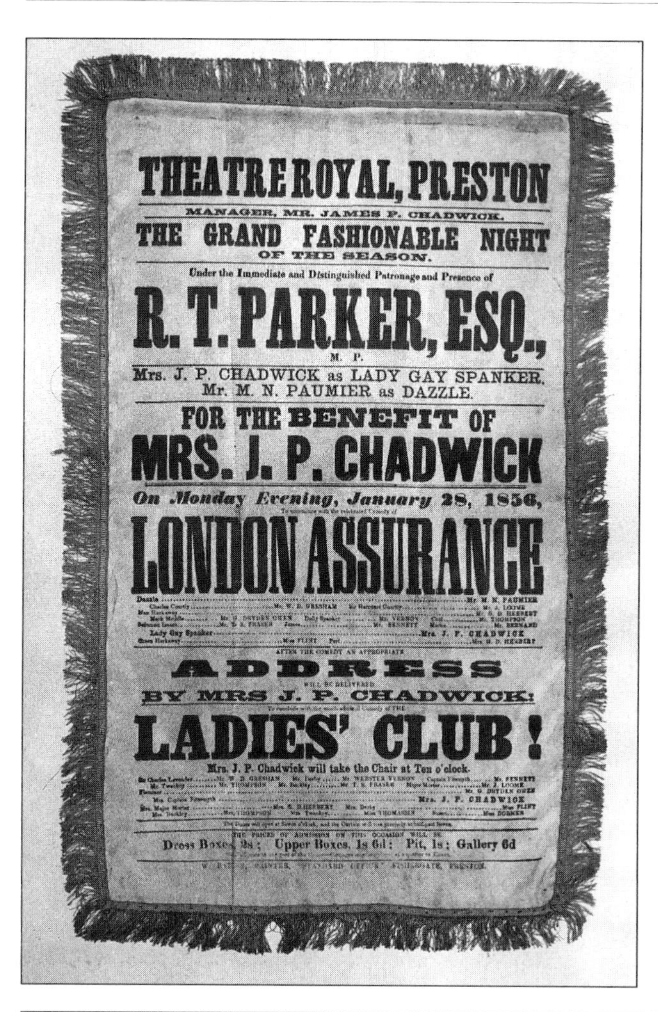

This Theatre Royal souvenir programme of 1856 was printed on silk for a special grand fashionable night. It was around this time that Victorian novelist Charles Dickens appeared at the theatre to perform one of his readings from the stage. The theatre was in Fishergate and was demolished in 1956 and rebuilt as the ABC Cinema.

The Preston Playhouse in Market Street was known as the Columba Dance Hall prior to World War Two. In its earlier days it had been a Quaker chapel.

The Empire in Church Street ceased as a cinema in 1964 to become a bingo palace before it was demolished and rebuilt as a store.

One of the early 1920s Empire Theatre programmes before it became a cinema.

Preston's shortest-lived picture house, the ABC, was demolished in 1986 only 27 years after its fanfare trumpet opening. The site became part of the Fishergate Centre.

The Palladium, Church Street, was opposite the Ritz Cinema, and was first opened in 1915. For many years the same company owned both cinemas.

Preston's last town centre cinema, the Odeon, which closed in 1991 had three different names and internal alterations. It began in 1928 as the New Victoria, showing silent films. After the war it became the Gaumont and then the Odeon.

This is how the Odeon luxury auditorium looked when the balcony had been removed in 1965 after it had been changed from the Gaumont.

And this is how it looked a short time later when the luxury auditorium ceiling collapsed! Fortunately, it happened after the cinema had closed for the night and no one was injured.

The Continental Cinema, in Tunbridge Street, was formerly the Queen's Cinema

The *Lancashire Daily Post's* Guardian Office building at 127 Fishergate, as it looked in 1936. In 1949 the newspaper reverted to its original title of *Lancashire Evening Post.*

And here's how it looked in 1989 shortly before production was transferred to Oliver's Place Fulwood.

The 1902 Guild Trades procession in North Road. In the right foreground is Moor Lane corner.

This huge archway dominated Plungington Road at the corner of Havelock Street in the 1902 Guild. The view is looking southwards downhill.

Civic dignitaries at the junction of Church Street and Lancaster Road head for the Parish Church in the 1902 Guild.

Frilly dress was clearly the fashion in the 1902 Guild. Boots Chemists, Fishergate, is now at the forefront right.

Pomp and ceremony as 1922 Guild Mayor Alderman Astley-Bell is escorted to the Parish Church.

Umbrellas were being used by the watchers as sun-shades when this religious procession in the 1922 Guild went along Stanley Street. The bandsmen are wearing a mixture of uniforms, bowler hats, flat caps and suits.

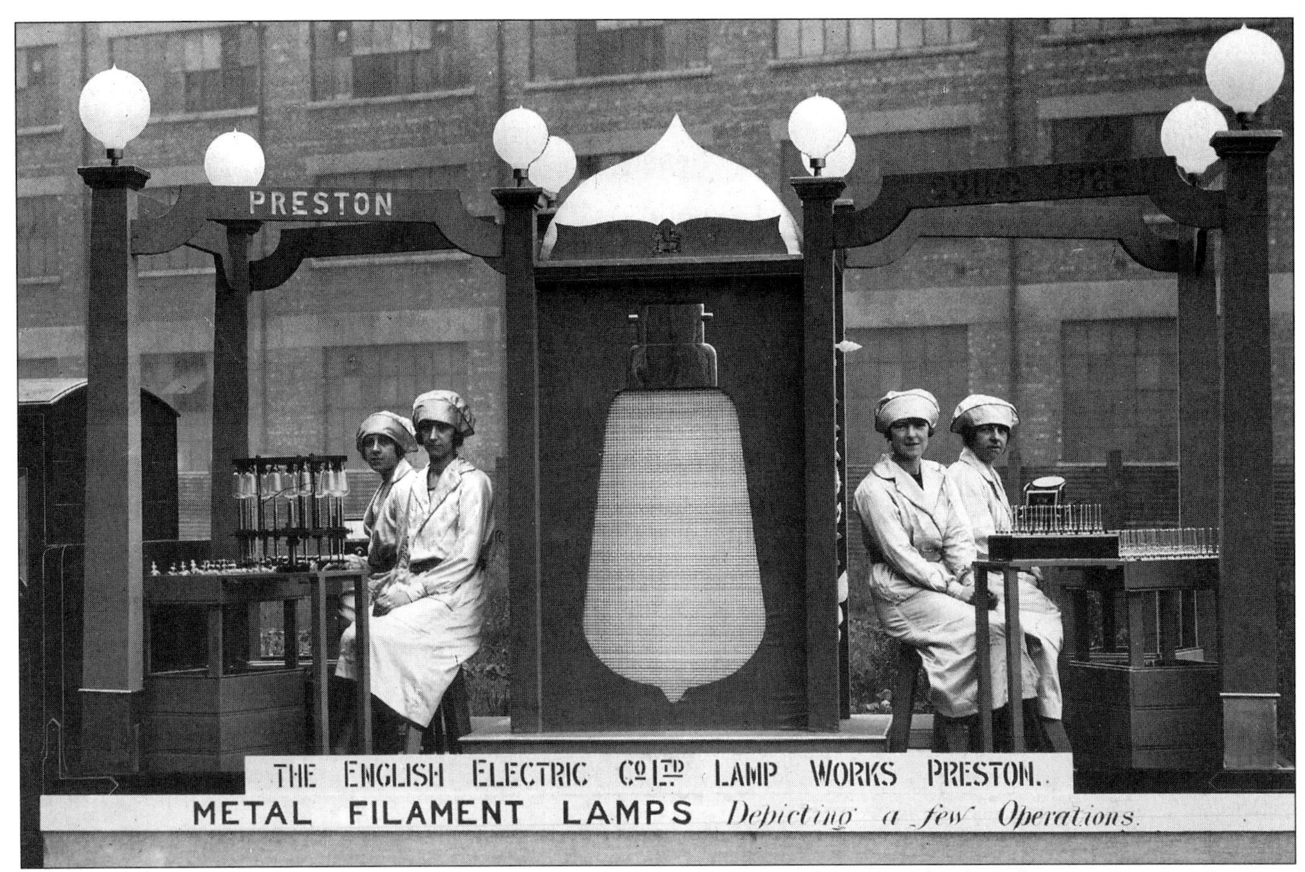

English Electric Lamp Co's 1922 Guild tableau outside the Watery Lane factory which later became Siemens Lamps.

A textile tableau passing under the bales of the cotton arch outside Horrocks' HQ (left) in Stanley Street in the 1922 Guild.

Horse transport still outnumbered motor vehicle transport in the 1922 Trades procession in Church Street.

A pause in the procession. The Sunday Schools section halts in Ribbleton Lane at the corner of Deepdale Road in the 1922 Guild.

Part of the crowd at the top of London Road waiting for one of the 1922 Guild processions to pass. Cheetham Arms is on the right.

The butcher's cap is a few sizes too big, but he doesn't seem to mind as he displays the Scotch Beef Butchers' Association exhibit in the 1922 Trades procession.

Preston Sea Cadets passing C.W.Mallotts, plumbers, and Stanley Garage in New Hall Lane in the 1922 Guild.

1952 Guild Mayor Mr J.J.Ward and the Mayoress receive the Town Hall tower model and scrolls from a runner, just prior to the opening of the week's Guild ceremonies. The scrolls had been sent to the main cities of the Commonwealth for exiled Prestonians to sign.

The opening of the 1952 Guild Court in the Public Hall.

Snap! The Amalgamated Society of Woodworkers' banner breaks in the strong winds during the 1952 Guild. Note the bus shelters here in Jacson Street.

These cotton girl workers in the 1952 Guild Trades procession display their hopes in the fading textile industry. The shops in the background, in Fishergate, have since been replaced by Debenhams store.

St James' Church was well represented in the 1952 Guild.

Horses still played a useful role in the 1952 Free Churches Guild processions and schoolboys still wore short trousers!

The 1952 Guild torchlight procession to Avenham Park provided lots of fun.

All decorated up for the 1952 Guild. These are the neighbours of Gordon Street, between Adelphi Street and Brook Street. In the distance is the former Hawkins mill and factory-link bridge. The massive chimney can be seen above the house roofs. It was the tallest in Preston.

Floyer Street, off London Road, was a prizewinner as one of the best decorated streets in the 1952 Guild.

The 1972 Guild Trades procession in Fishergate.

Mersey Street neighbours were in high spirits as award winners in the 1972 Guild best decorated street contest.

A turning point in the 1972 Guild in Garstang Road. On the right now is Canterbury Hall.

Preston at Work

Dick, Kerr's East Works, looking eastwards, from the Dock Estate around 1900. West Works (still standing) was built later.

Noon break for Dick, Kerr workers in Strand Road in 1910. The clock tower was demolished around World War One. This view is from the Marsh Lane end. West Works (left) is now GEC factory.

One of English Electrics early aircraft products at Preston in 1923. The little Wren aeroplane was single-engined.

Gearing up for war. In November 1938, English Electric began to extend their works for producing the Hampden twin-engine bomber. The chimney and tower of Wellfield Mill can be seen (left) and the old Spa Road Mill chimney (centre).

One of the earliest Preston buildings to be requisitioned by the government in 1939 was Vineys Transport which was next to the English Electric Co in Strand Road. The white-painted kerbstones were a guide in the black-outs.

The same view in 1940 as the extension progresses.

And the same view in 1941 – which had then become the Halifax bomber assembly section. In 1994 all this was ruthlessly swept away when British Aerospace pulled out.

In June 1940, construction was started on English Electrics site on the former Wellfield Road mill. In the background St Mark's (left) and St Walburge's (right).

Stephenson's foundry in Fylde Road was being used in 1944 by English Electric for aircraft production. The building later became part of Thorn Lighting.

A team of USSR air officials visit Samlesbury airfield in 1944 to inspect the latest Halifax bombers made in Preston.

Part of the Halifax bomber assembly plant at English Electric, Preston.

An official inspection of Halifax bomber production at English Electric, Strand Road, during the war.

The first picture to be released in 1954 of English Electrics highly successful Canberra MK B6, details of which were then top secret.

Prime Minister ("Not the pound in your pocket") Harold Wilson signs the visitors book in the Mayor's Parlour with the Mayor and Mayoress, Councillor Joe and Mrs Lund, looking on. After Harold Wilson became Prime Minister in 1964 the Government scrapped the plans for English Electric's controversial TSR2 aircraft which was to have been made in Preston.

GEC publicity manager in 1975, Norman Gardener (left) shows an Egyptian rail chief around the Strand Road works with manager Sam Fawthorpe (right). This factory used to be part of Dick, Kerr's tram works.

Dryden's foundry in Grimshaw Street, Preston, was run by the family for three generations starting in 1871. In 1944 it was bought by Coxleys and then Deveres, but still traded as Dryden's. It closed in 1974.

Lostock Hall Gasworks as it looked in 1932 – a mere fraction of the size it was later to become. Then, when North Sea gas replaced coal gas, its size diminished again.

No, it's not Chernobyl nuclear plant ready to explode! It's Lostock Hall coal and gas works as it looked in an autumn sunset in 1970.

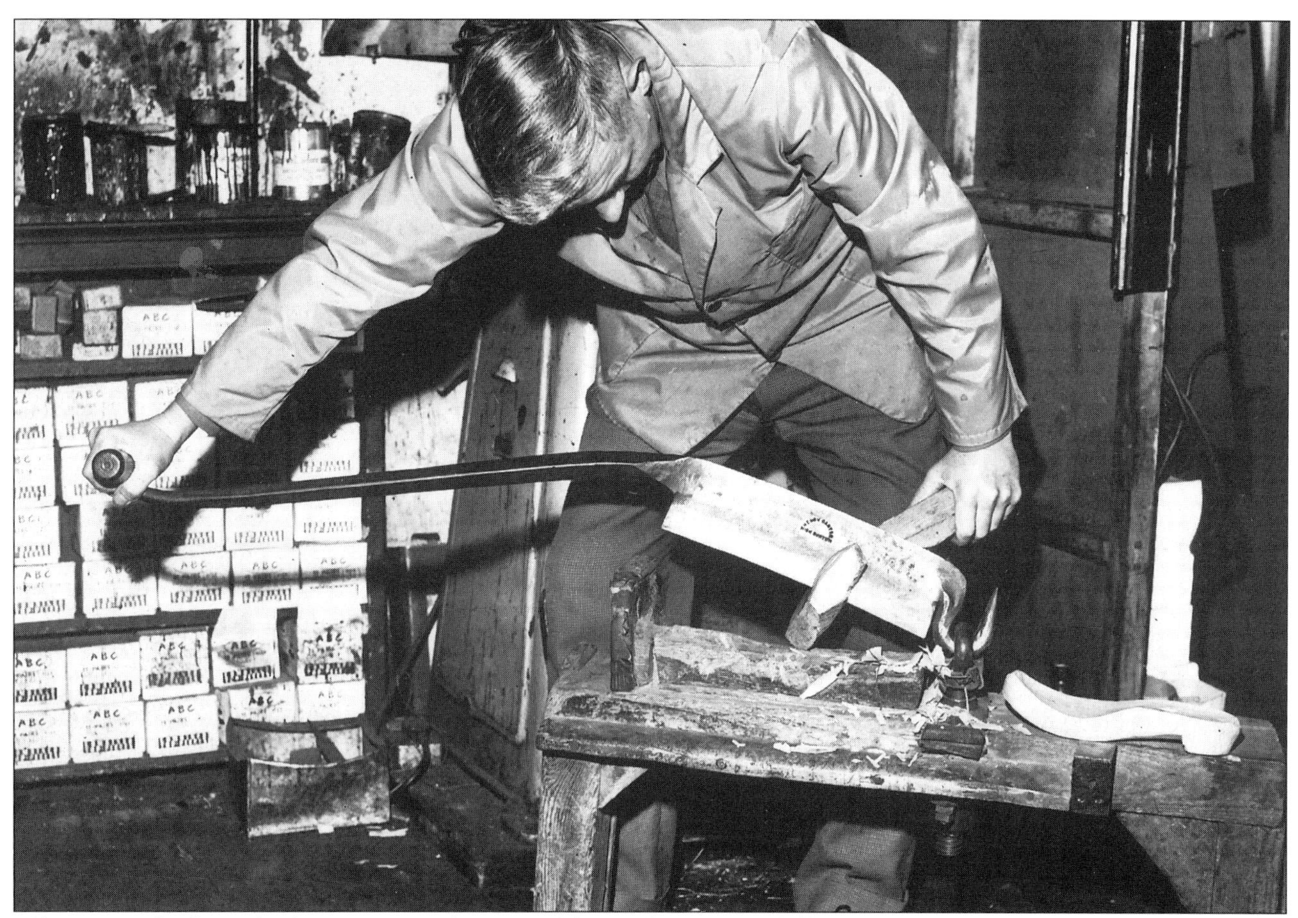

Clogs were the favourite footwear once for Lancashire workers – especially cotton mill operatives. Here a clog maker shapes a clog sole out of a wooden block.

A foundry worker in 1936 shaping clog irons which were sold to local cloggers.

Clog irons are shown here ready for placing in the coal furnace for the annealing process.

A cold spell in 1956 saw some people on the look out for the once familiar Lancashire clogs which were always noted for keeping feet warm and dry.

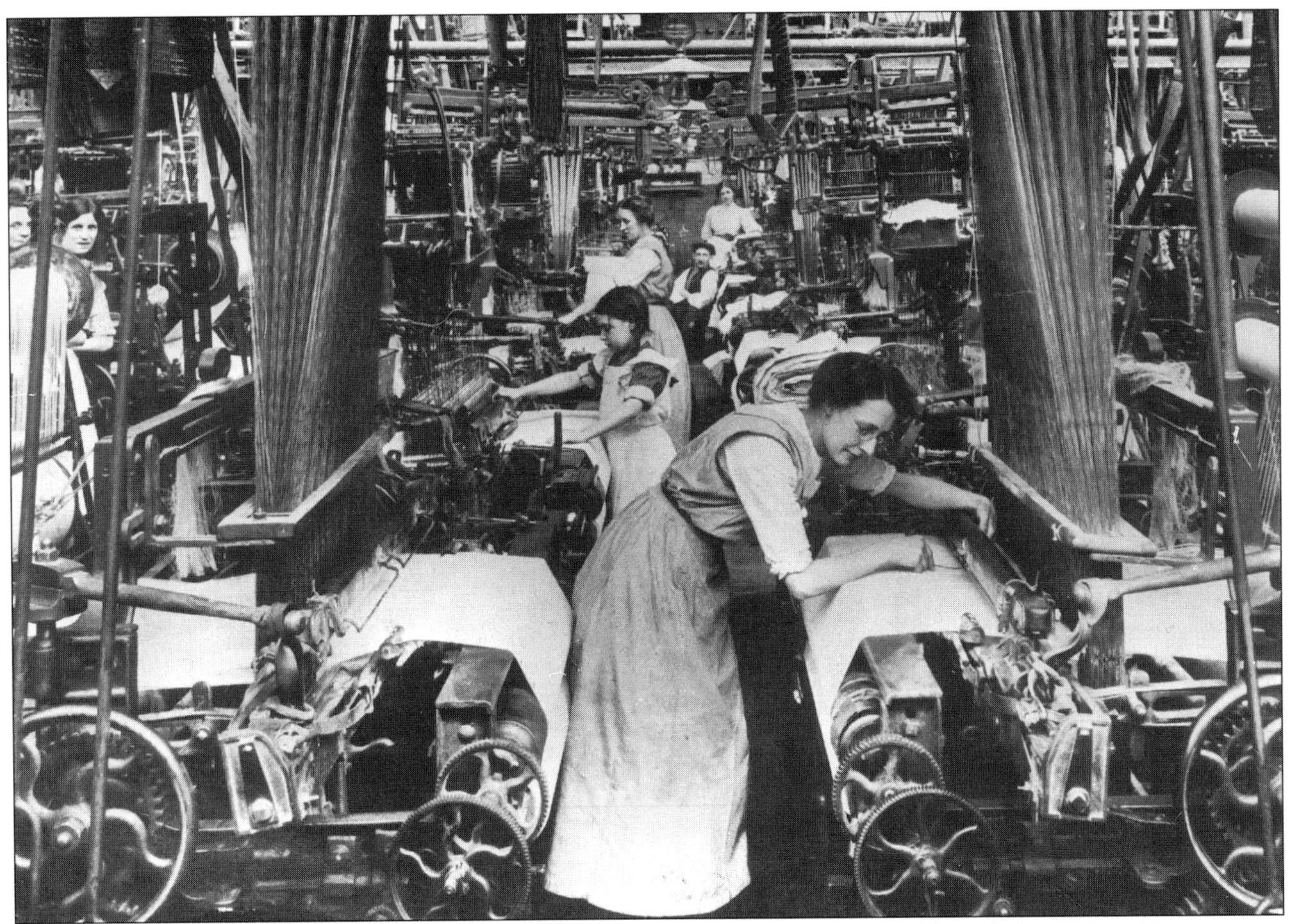

Weavers at Horrocks' Crewdson Mill in 1900. Among them is the young girl aged about 12 or 13.

Cotton mill women at J & A Leigh's Brookhouse Mill all trimmed up for the 1902 Preston Guild. Notice the old grannies still working as there were no old age benefits then.

The Hungry Thirties! Preston chief constable J.P.Kerr Watson gives out Christmas food parcels to the unemployed in 1932 from money raised by the police. Note, each recipient politely doffs his cap.

Cotton workers moving beams at Horrocks' Crewdson Mill, Preston, seem happy at their work in 1935.

This rare 1919 aerial photo shows Tulketh Mill before it became surrounded by streets. The picture was taken looking eastwards. The dark line across the centre is the railway. The houses to the right near the top of the chimney are in Brook Street in front of the Cattle Market and the curve on the left of the picture is Lytham Road, vanishing beneath the railway.

Putting the finishing touch to Tulketh Mill chimney. No longer a cotton mill, but it still has its chimney.

Shelley Road old cotton mill is still there today – along with the tower – but the tall chimney has since gone.

This tall, proud chimney at Bute Mill, Essex Street, off St Paul's Road, has now gone the way of many others. Deepdale rail track is seen bottom left.

Emerson Mill, Ribbleton, built in 1907 and closed in 1965.

Another factory chimney slowly disappears brick by brick. This time it is the Fishwick Dye Works overlooking Brockholes view. The factory once belonged to Horrocks'.

This is how Courtaulds first began searching for water in 1933 when they planned to build their factory at Red Scar. They employed Douglas Walton, of Bretherton, a water diviner, to locate an underground supply with his hazel twig divining rod.

Two giant 360ft-high chimneys at Courtaulds Red Scar works were felled in 1983. Watching them fall were three retired sad bricklayers who helped to build them as young men. One said, "It took a lot of hard work to put them up. I can hardly bear to watch."

No women were employed in Preston Savings Bank (now TSB) in Church Street when this was taken, somewhere around 1920.

Inside Preston General Post Office in 1932. The counter assistants each dealt with individual postal items, *eg* one section for stamps, another for postal orders etc. This public office was moved round the corner into Birley Street in the 1970s and reorganised.

No postal codes or computerised letter-sorting here in 1936 as workers cope with the Christmas rush, yet the GPO could guarantee a letter posted in Preston by 8pm would be delivered in London next day.

Siemens Lamps in Strand Road opened in 1923. At the peak of production they employed 1,100 people, mostly females. In 1946 the firm opened a factory in Fylde Road. By 1981 both factories had been closed down. These were some of the women at Siemens in 1958.

Thos Harrison's bakery in Hermon Street used to supply much of the Preston area with bread and confectionery. It was started in a small bakery in 1840 and was run by Spillers Limited when it closed down in 1978.

Port of Preston

This rare 1863 picture shows part of Ashton Marsh. It was taken from Whinfield, the home of Edmund Harris. The river's course was diverted in 1884 to the base of the hill on the far right to make way for the construction of Preston Dock. Ashton Marsh was a popular gathering ground for sports. The lane in the centre is now busy Riversway.

Graceful sailing ships arrived in Preston Dock until the late 1920s. These three are moored on the north side of the port around 1910.

The dock foundation stone being laid by Prince Albert Edward of Wales on 17 July 1885. The official name of the port is the Albert Edward Dock.

Concrete ships were built in 1919 on this slipway just outside Preston Dock entrance on the riverside. This is the *Cretemanor*, almost ready for launching. The ships were a failure. In the 1970s another firm tried a similar venture which also failed.

Surfaced again! Here is the actual stone in the dock wall which only became visible again after the port was closed to large ships. Throughout the years the port was open, the stone was constantly beneath the surface due to the water displacement caused by the weight of the ships.

It took three salvage attempts to raise the corporation tug *Penfold* after she sank one night in the dock in 1950. Fortunately, no one was aboard at the time. Her wheelhouse and mast are showing above the surface, The *Walter Bibby* and *Savick* were two corporation dredgers.

Preston Dock had its own diver from its earliest days. This picture was taken in 1906 and this type of diving equipment was still in use at the dock in the 1960s.

Dock diver Jack Bell entering the murky waters to try and put a cable beneath the *Penfold* in a bid to salvage her.

The tug *Penfold* moored in the Ribble after she had been salvaged. The men aboard are looking for the cause of her sinking.

A lady tramp! The most well known of all the tramp steamers to sail regularly into the dock was the *Helen Craig*. She brought her first cargo to Preston before the dock was opened and moored at a riverside wharf. She was given a momentous civic farewell and every ship in the dock gave her an emotional siren blast as she sailed for the breakers' yard in 1959. Her skipper for most of the time was Captain Kennedy.

The Preston Corporation dredger *Arpley* belching out smoke on the River Ribble. Dredgers were in constant use to clear the channel of sand washed in by the tides from the Irish Sea.

Cargo ships from the USSR in 1965, moored in Preston Dock. Despite the Cold War, they often sailed into the port, but the crews were seldom allowed to go ashore. In 1962, one 21-year-old deserted and obtained political asylum in Britain.

Severe damage was caused by fire in 1964 when the Soviet ship *Igarkales* (right), bringing timber to Preston Dock, caught fire. A special tug (seen here alongside the *Igarkales*) was sent from Russia to tow the vessel home.

The Soviet ship *Igarkales* on fire. Preston firemen are seen fighting the blaze.

Water from this corner of the dock basin used to flow through a huge tunnel under the River Ribble to the Power Station on the Penwortham side. The Power Station was demolished around 1978.

A sturdy tramp steamer glides down the Ribble passing the mouth of the River Douglas on its way to the ocean.

This tragic ship *Druid* sank in the Ribble estuary trying to reach Preston Dock during a storm in 1962. Three of the crew perished and three were saved. Here she is seen moored in the Ribble after being salvaged.

The Preston Dock bonded warehouse on Strand Road was built in 1845 and pulled down in 1983 (just after this picture was taken) to make way for the new traffic bridge over the Ribble.

Marooned: in June, 1952 a mussel gatherer off Lytham took refuge on one of Preston Corporation Dock river channel beacons after being cut off by the tide.

Rescued: a boatman later sailed to the beacon and saved him.

The year 1948 saw the start of a big change which was to affect the dock trade. It was the inauguration of the first roll-on roll-off lorry service between Preston and Larne. By 1956 there were seven of these vessels operating from the port. Here is one of them, *Empire Nordic*, with loaded lorries which had been driven aboard.

The dock trade was falling rapidly by the time this photograph was taken in 1972. It shows Fiat cars being driven off the shallow draft-car transport *Montlhery* which had just arrived from Italy.

The dock ceased as a port in 1981. After that demolition of many of the buildings got under way. This granary had belonged to the firm of Joseph Pyke Limited, who had operated at the dock since well before the turn of the century. The suction elevation could hold 3,500 tons of imported grain. Demolition gangs reduced it to rubble in 1985.

Transport and Waterways

They were made to last! This tram, built by Preston's Dick, Kerr works, was still in use in Japan in 1987. The company's trams were exported all over the world.

All set for a great day out. It may have been a rough ride in a charabanc with solid tyres on cobbled roads, but this club outing around 1925 didn't seem to mind. Who said heated and air-conditioned coaches were a must!

Deepdale Road was widened around 1930 to make it safer and to cut out a bottleneck caused by the tram-track on the left. The old Sumners Hotel can be seen at the top of the hill.

A double-deck tramcar in Fishergate in 1933 takes up the centre of the road. No car-parking problems, yellow lines or traffic wardens to bother about then.

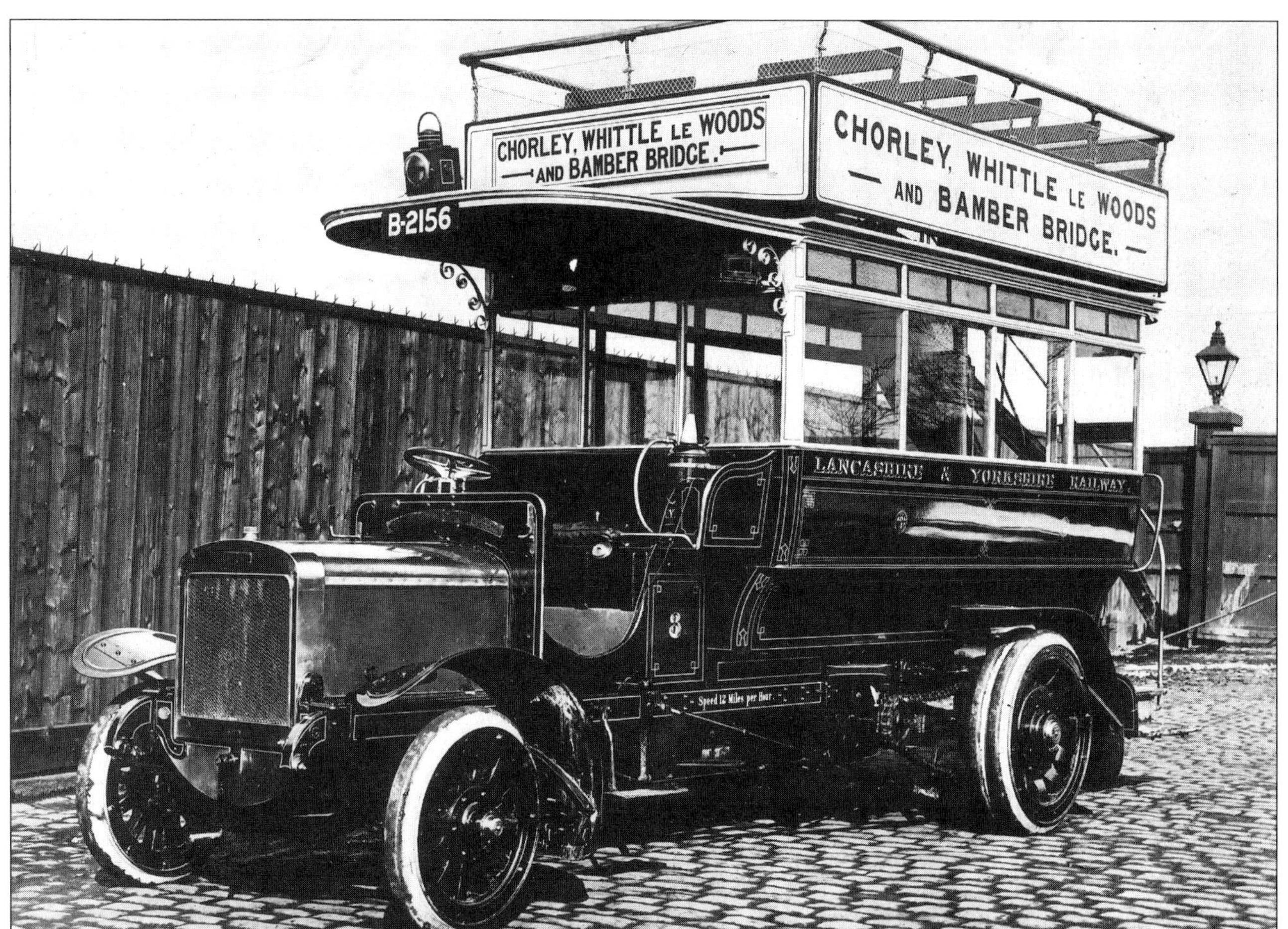

This solid tyred bone-shaker was owned by Lancashire & Yorkshire Railway and ran between Bamber Bridge and Chorley.

This Ribble golden oldie was a Leyland Lion built in 1927. The engine was fired by the heavy starting-handle at the front.

Tithebarn Street Ribble bus station was generally approached from narrow alleyway in Lancaster Road called Ward's End which is to the right, near the telegraph pole. The large building is the Empire Cinema.

Hardings were among the biggest cab owners in Preston in Victorian and Edwardian days. This is their stable in the Old Vicarage, off Tithebarn Street.

Here are the same stables in 1930 when they were owned by Merigold Bros as their motor car garage and showroom.

The Ribble bus station was replaced by the present bus station in 1969. The Empire Hotel can been seen left.

The old Ribble bus station as seen from the Cheetham Street end.

Holidays abroad went no further than the Isle of Man for this large crowd on Preston Railway Station in 1950. The queue is for the boat-train for Fleetwood during Preston holiday week which was then held in August when the town virtually closed down.

Stand back, it's coming. This photograph appeared in the *Evening Post* on 22 July 1957, which was then the start of Preston's annual holiday week. A report in the *Post* said that, in contrast, the bus station that day had been nearly deserted, which showed that rail travel was still the most popular.

Bond Minicars made in Ribbleton, Preston, made their first appearance in 1950. A three-wheeler, it had a Villiers 125cc two-stroke engine and did up to 100 miles to a gallon of petrol. It had a roll-back canvas hood, and was the answer to European bubble cars.

This was the 1954 Bond Mini, 197cc engine, capable of also carrying two youngsters in the rear.

The 1958 Bond Mk E which did 85 mpg. In 1962 the government dropped purchase tax on all four-wheel cars from 45 per cent to 25 per cent, but no similar deduction was given to the lower taxed three-wheelers. This was a blow for the Bond and the factory closed down after making a total of 100,000 small vehicles.

Who are these people proudly walking along the M6 motorway, indeed! None other than Prime Minister ("You've never had it so good") Harold Macmillan and other VIPs making their way in December 1958, to unveil the commemorative plaque at Samlesbury Bridge marking the historic opening of part of Britain's first motorway. The Prime Minister then drove along the completed section which ended at Broughton roundabout.

A fright for motorists. In January 1979, when motorists saw this it quickly led to the next scene.

Queuing up for petrol on London Road in 1979. All caused by fuel tanker and lorry drivers going on strike in midwinter for a 25 per cent pay increase. Lack of oil caused many petrol stations and schools to close. Bus services ceased to run and the disruption lasted a week.

Few towns are more favourably situated than Preston for the advantages of pleasure boating on a fairly wide tidal river. Boating here was popular until around 1950 then, sadly, Cootons boathouse ceased, never to be replaced. Around 1910, when this picture was taken, it belonged to Crooks.

Two graveyards – one for mankind and a distant one for ships. This unusual 1950 view from Penwortham churchyard shows a vessel moored in the Ribble ready to be broken up at Ward's shipbreakers. The overhead gantry conveyed coal from the Dock to Penwortham Power Station.

Life seemed placid and carefree for bargees and their families who lived and worked on the Preston-Lancaster Canal. This idyllic scene in 1900 of the horse-drawn barge is near the Lea swing-bridge.

The low canal bridge arches were regularly whitewashed when barges plied the waterway to ensure that the bargees were aware of the overhang.

This well-groomed animal was said to be Preston's oldest working horse in the 1930s. It was owned by Thos Banks and Co at their Fletcher Road coalyard where they are still in business today.

A 1960s view of the canal basin taken from the footbridge off Tulketh Brow. St Mark's Church tower is in the distance. A old barge lies sunken in the reeds.

A thirsty milk-cart horse! Horse troughs were not uncommon at one time in Preston streets. This was the last to remain after World War Two. It was at the entrance to the Cattle Market in Brook Street.

What's this? Two bus drivers for one bus! In case you may have forgotten, every bus had a conductor whose job was to give the travelling passengers their tickets. And from his leather bag he gave change, too, if you needed it!

Parks, Baths, Markets and Leisure

A graceful summer Victorian scene in Miller Park. Sunday afternoon strolls were popular along this walk with the wealthier classes. The presence of poorer dressed working folk was frowned upon.

The Old Tram Bridge, Avenham Park, being redecked in 1966. It was first built in 1802 to carry wagons of coal from the Leeds-Liverpool Canal at Walton Summit. It ceased as a tramway in 1859, as the railways took over. Severe floods in 1937 damaged the original oak pillars and they were later replaced by similar concrete ones.

The winding shaft which used to haul the coal trucks up Avenham Park slope from the Old Tram Bridge.

Rowing used to be popular on the River Ribble between the Old Tram Bridge and Penwortham Old Bridge. This photograph was taken on an Easter Monday in the 1930s showing queues waiting to sail. The boathouse closed down around 1950.

Not many people have seen this ornamental piece of volcanic basalt rock from Giant'‘s Causeway, Northern Ireland, which is sited in a Miller Park plantation.

Another stone – the 'Starting Chair' stone still to be seen in Moor Park. It was first used in the Preston Moor horse races of 1726. The Observatory is in the background.

Children love to splash and this warm summer day in June, 1960 was no exception. The once-popular kiddies' paddling and boating pool beside the Moor Park Serpentine was later neglected and abandoned.

The old Observatory built in 1881 in Deepdale Road was replaced in 1927 by the present one in Moor Park.

Moor Park Observatory creator G.G.Gibbs prepares his camera for the sensational 1927 total eclipse of the sun which plunged Britain into darkness during daytime. Thousands gathered on the park to watch it.

The first Saul Street Baths were opened in 1851 consisting of this pool and a much smaller one. Dressing cubicles were on two floors and water often dripped through the rough wooden floorboards on to the clothes of the bathers below. Mixed bathing was forbidden. There were separate days for males and females. These baths closed in 1936.

When the old Saul Street Baths first opened, the public were allowed to use one part (seen here) to wash their clothes. In 1870 this washing service ceased, as laundries began to open elsewhere in the town.

Saul Street Baths, combined with the Queen's Hall, was opened in 1936. It had two pools – one large (seen here) and one small. In its earlier years the large pool was boarded over in winter and used as a ballroom. The baths were demolished in 1991 to make way for the construction of the new Crown Court.

Haslam Park open-air baths in 1958.

Waverley Park open-air baths in Ribbleton which finally closed in 1979. This is how they looked in 1958.

Moor Park open-air baths when it closed down in 1971.

The tumbling boats were popular with the youngsters for many years at Preston's Whitsuntide Fair.

Preston's traditional Whitsuntide Fair had always lasted from Friday until Tuesday night (except for Sunday). Around 1960 the council decided to restrict the fair to Saturday and Monday because of complaints that the crowds caused traffic problems.

Children gather around the balloon seller at Preston's Whitsuntide Fair.

Boxing booths and freak shows used to be part of the attractions of the Whitsuntide fairground. Lostock Hall boxer, Jack McCabe, is in the centre, ready to take on all comers.

This was a scene from Preston's Whitsuntide Fair in June 1946. Judging by the number of raincoats being worn it was clearly an unsettled one for weather.

WAREING'S
UNIQUE
AMBROSE'S

Isn't she a pretty girl! There was a spot of May sunshine for the 1948 Whitsun Fair.

The ice-cream vendors of long ago were proud of their home-made product and gaudily painted vehicles. The Italian brothers, Luigi, Raffaele and Dominic Terribile outside their Adelphi Street shop in 1923.

All dressed up and ready for the crowds. Stallholders have it all prepared for the ancient Pot Fair in 1900.

Preston Pot Fair fire in August 1931 is still talked about. The blaze was started unintentionally by two small boys playing with matches on a hot but quiet Sunday afternoon. Every stall was damaged.

The Preston Pot Fair still attracts customers, and there is clear evidence here, in 1937, that no woman shopper would be seen without wearing a hat.

Every Saturday morning outside the Public Hall (now the Corn Exchange) a livestock and produce market used to be held, patronised by country and townsfolk. This is the scene around 1935 when it was called the Butter Market.

The same Saturday morning market viewed from Lune Street where eggs, poultry, cheese and pet animals were sold. The Wharf Street buildings (far side) were cleared in 1963 for Ringway. The Public Hall canopy was removed around 1939.

Stalls were allowed on the Market Square on Saturdays, but this market ceased after the new Market Hall opened around 1971. When this picture was taken in 1949, stockings, like other clothing, were rationed.

Windy days played havoc for stallholders on the Saturday Market Square trading. This was the result of a gale in October 1935.

Car boot stalls and flea markets were unheard of in 1949, but the occasional second-hand stall was still attracting custom. This area was also the Fish Market as well in those days.

Preston at War

As soon as World War One broke out on 4 August 1914, thousands of young men in the Preston area rushed to join the Forces. Here they are seen cheerfully queuing at the Railway Station little realising the horrors and carnage they would soon be facing on the Western Front.

A hero's welcome – Preston's World War One Victoria Cross hero was Private William Young. He received the award from the King for saving his wounded officer under fire in France. Here he is seen at Preston Town Hall with his wife and nine children. Sadly, he died later from the effects of his wounds.

A hero's farewell. The military funeral of Private Young from his terraced home in Heysham Street, next to Adelphi Street. The flag-draped coffin is borne on a gun-carriage to Preston Cemetery.

Private Young's Victoria Cross was officially handed to the Queen's Lancashire Regiment in 1985. Mr William Young (left), the VC's son, and his great-nephew are holding the award.

Left: Hero No.2 – Preston's second Victoria Cross hero was Jim Towers. He also won the award in World War One when he crawled into the German lines under heavy fire and rescued his encircled comrades. He lived into his 80s. Here he is seen at Preston Cenotaph shortly before he died. Right: Bamber Bridges' hero. An appeal was made by Walton-le-Dale Urban Council in 1918 for contributions to help the widow and four children of Corporal John McNamara who was awarded the Victoria Cross for gallantry in France. John was shot dead by a German sniper only three weeks before World War One ended and he never knew he had won Britain's highest award for bravery. His home was in School Lane, Bamber Bridge.

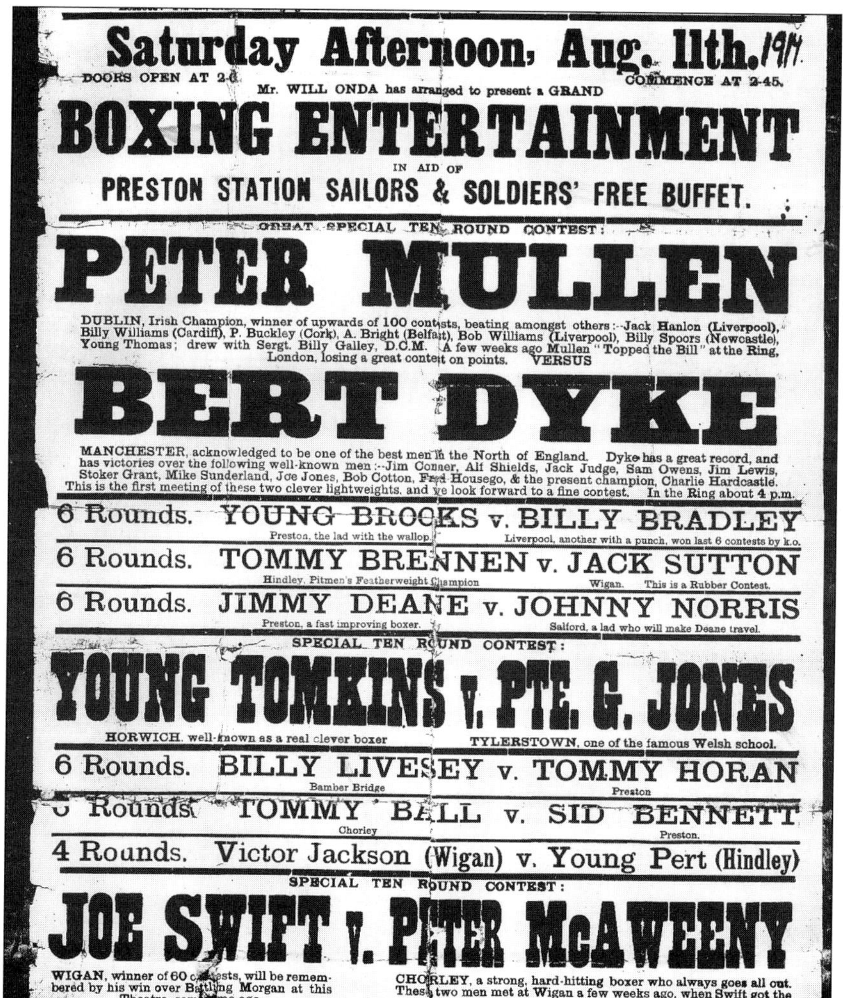

A 1917 boxing tournament poster for an event staged at the Prince's Theatre in aid of Preston Station Sailors' and Soldiers' Free Buffet. The RAF had not then been formed and airmen were linked with the Army in the Royal Flying Corps.

How to fire a field gun. Volunteers in the 88th Territorial Field Regiment at Stanley Street Drill Hall in 1938 receive expert instruction. Most of these 'Terriers' were taken prisoner by the Japanese at Singapore in 1941. Tragically, many died through ill-treatment.

Just before the outbreak of World War Two, valuable paintings and exhibits in the Harris Art Gallery were taken to places of safety. Councillor J.Harrison and Sydney Paviere, the curator, watch the removals in August 1939.

Fortunately no air attacks were made on Preston Royal Infirmary during World War Two. These sandbags were placed on the roof of the operating theatre in September 1939.

The wartime shortage of sweets is clearly in evidence here with this sympathetic shopkeeper telling the disappointed little girl and her mum that the sweet jars and shelves are all empty. Sweet rationing was introduced in June 1942.

Many wounded soldiers evacuated from Dunkirk in May-June 1940 were conveyed by rail to Preston and then by ambulance to Whittingham Hospital, part of which became a military hospital during World War Two.

One of the Lostock Hall air-raids. This was the scene when a German daylight bomber raided the Ward Street-Princes Street area in October 1940. The bombs were intended for nearby Leyland Motors. The total killed in this attack was 25, including a complete family.

Air-raid wardens continue the search for victims in the Lostock Hall daylight raid in October 1940.

The cloisters on Preston's old Town Hall were sand-bagged to protect the part of the building which housed the Food Office which issued the public's ration books.

There's nothing like a cup of char for a spot of cheer! WVS workers from Preston Station Free Buffet greet a passing troop train with buckets of tea and baskets of buns. The buffet was known throughout the land for kindness in providing free refreshments to all servicemen passing through the station. It was staffed by volunteers 24 hours daily throughout the war and financed by local fund-raising efforts.

Hold that picture! This innocent-looking snow-scene photograph was taken on 20 February 1941, in Avenham Park, but the *Lancashire Daily Post* was forbidden to publish it until two weeks later, on 3 March. This was part of the wartime censorship on the weather reports to deny the Germans up-to-date information.

These women working in the old Town Hall are engaged in preparing the food ration books which the public had to queue for every few months until long after the war was over.

This German Messerschmitt – one of many shot down over Britain in World War Two – was used to promote war savings campaigns. This one with the Nazi swastika shot away on the tail-rudder was sited for a time on the Market Square. Note the brick air-raid shelters on the edge of the square.

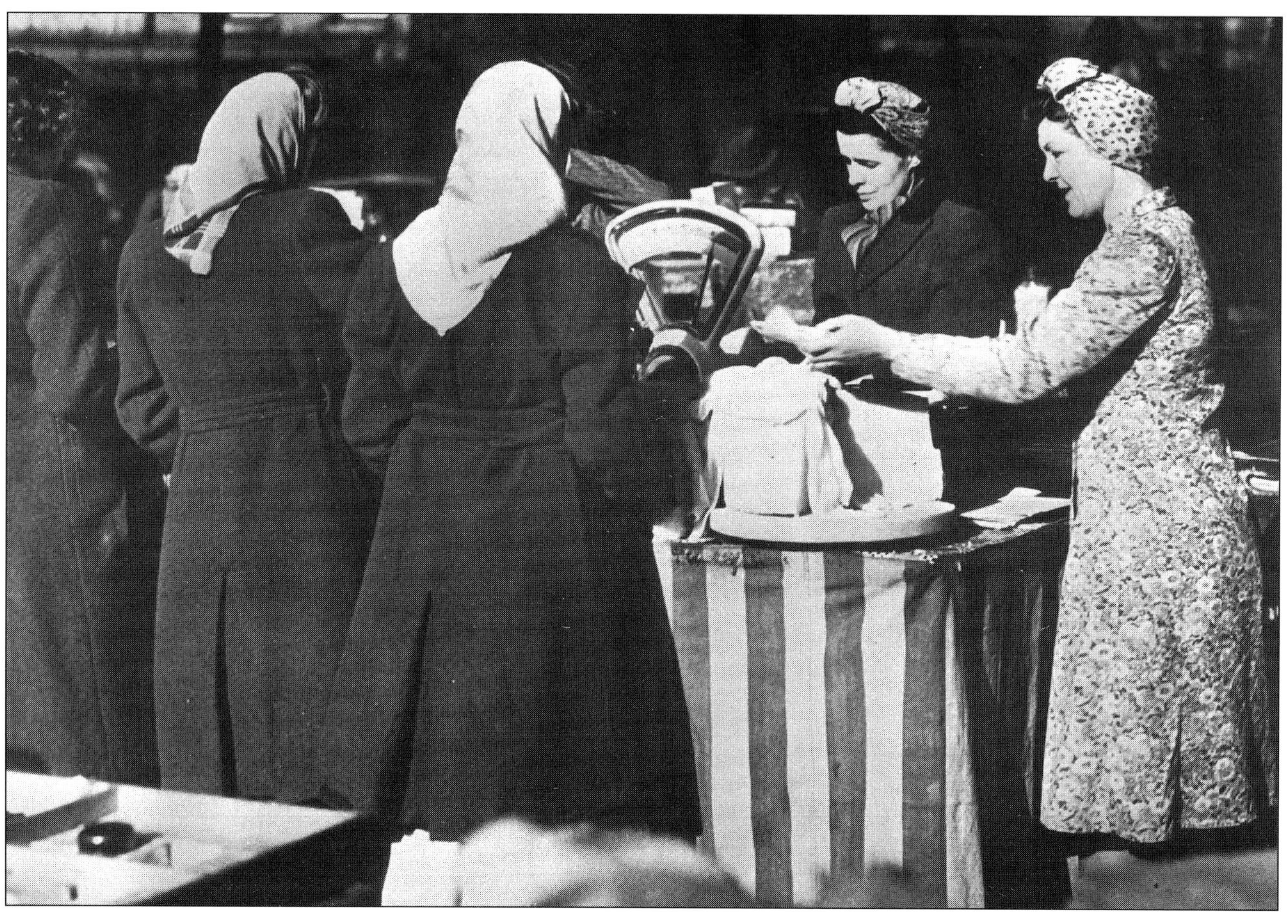

Women in head scarves were a common sight in wartime. These women on Preston covered market are buying the meagre weekly cheese ration.

The *Liseta* petrol tanker after she blew up in Preston Dock in 1943 killing the captain and seven crew. The death toll would have been greater had the other 44 crewmen not gone ashore minutes before. The explosion was an accident and the blast rocked the town.

The Home Guard performed invaluable work during the war. Here they are being inspected on Avenham Park by a high-ranking officer.

This building was used by English Electric Co during the war as a shadow factory in the building of Halifax bombers. Several of these secret factories were scattered throughout the town in case the Strand Road works was bombed. Note the security man at the door and the concrete blocks to obstruct possible invasion tanks. The road direction sign on the right lamp standard would have been removed later. The building is in Fishergate opposite Butler Street.

During the war the Government encouraged 'Stay at Home' holidays. A fairground on Moor Park was one of the features of Preston's 1944 August Holiday Week.

The Home Guard's final parade in Preston on being officially stood down took place in November 1944. Taking the salute is Major-General G.Waterhouse, on his right is Alderman Walter Gordon and on his left is the Mayor, Councillor Gee.

Lancashire Daily Post.

No. 18,166 | REGISTERED AT THE GENERAL POST OFFICE AS A NEWSPAPER MONDAY, MAY 7, 1945 Published Daily, 1½d.

IT'S OVER : SURRENDER : COMPLETED

ORDER BY DOENITZ TO GERMAN FORCES

GENERALS SIGN AT EISENHOWER'S H.Q.

THE war in Europe is over. The Allies to-day officially announced that Germany had surrendered unconditionally, says a Rheims message.

The surrender took place at 2 41 a.m. (French time) to-day at Gen. Eisenhower's H.Q.

Col.-General Gustav Jodl, the new German Army Chief of Staff, signed for Germany.

General Bedell Smith, Eisenhower's Chief of Staff, signed for the Supreme Allied Command, according to an account of the ceremony broadcast by New York radio.

General Ivan Susoparoff signed for Russia and General Francois Sevez for France.

An earlier announcement from Flensburg, the

the years of war have found

PREMIER'S PLANS

The "Post" Political Correspondent says the end of the war in Europe will come with the signing of an instrument of surrender by the highest German authorities covering all pockets of resistance in Germany, in France, in Norway, the Channel Islands, and elsewhere.

The Prime Minister's announcement will be short, giving only the main facts. If he is able to give the first flash of the signing in the course of this afternoon or evening, the

MEN OF THE HOUR

"Stop" to U-Boats: Cabinet Waiting at Their Posts

NAZI TRICKS RIGHT TO THE END

By OUR DIPLOMATIC CORRESPONDENT.

THIS week-end really saw the end of German resistance, but on formal grounds the final surrender of the pitiful remnants of what was once the greatest military power in Europe—in the world perhaps—had to be postponed for a few hours.

The Allies wanted that last act of total submission accomplished in a manner rendering it impossible for the Germans to say later that in their death throes they succeeded in dividing the Big Three.

Norway, therefore, was singled out as a test case: the Western Allies deferred the acceptance of Doenitz's offer to surrender until the Nazi scapegoat agreed to extend his surrender simultaneously to the Russians.

Thus VE-Day is upon us. We should not mind Mr. Churchill bottling up that joyful news for a few hours longer if, by so doing, the Allies nip in the bud the enemy's attempt to make a show of surrendering to the Western Powers, while resistance continues to our Russian friends. That sort of typical German intrigue cannot be allowed.

NO LOOPHOLE

Only yesterday the alleged report of a non-existing German High Command headquarters announced that divisions fighting in the West had been transferred to the Eastern front to fight the Russians.

DEMPSEY IN COPENHAGEN

General Dempsey has arrived in Copenhagen. Kalunborg radio says arrival of Field Marshal Montgomery is expected.—"Post" London Service.

NEW YORK "WILD WITH JOY"

There were wild scenes of joy in New York within few minutes of receipt of Rheims message that Germany had surrendered unconditionally. Ticker tapes and bits of torn-up telephone books started fluttering down from skyscrapers in city's traditional manner of celebration.

LUFTWAFFE HELP R.A.F.

..The Luftwaffe flagged R.A.F. Dakota s into Copenhagen airfield on Saturday afternoon. Shortly afterwards air base and German garrison were formally surrendered to British forces.

WORLD WILL HEAR

The King's broadcast, and Mr. Churchill's on Thursday, will be heard throughout world on a scale never before equalled. Similar measures give fullest facilities in Britain to hear address of President Truman and other Allied leaders.

VICTORY SALVO

London may hear victory salvos on either VE-Day or VE-Day Plus One.

It's over: The *Daily Post* headline says it all. The news that peace-loving people everywhere had long waited for.

As soon as the BBC radio announced on the morning of 8 May 1945, that the Germans had surrendered, people made their way in thousands to the Market Square to share with each other the joyful news.

It did not take long for that vast crowd to break into joyful dancing and celebrating that day, thankful that the weary six-year European war was over at last.

Victory parade in Preston. The Army strides out on its march around town to celebrate the occasion. Here the troops are seen in Fishergate passing the Old Town Hall.

American GIs at their Red Cross Club in Glover's Court, Preston, invite British servicemen to join them in VE Day rejoicings. GIs were stationed at Ribbleton, Bamber Bridge, Warton and Chorley.

Bring out the bunting! Every street had its own way of expressing its happiness and relief that the war with Germany was over. This was in Allan Street, off Adelphi Street.

Cadley Causeway area residents celebrated VE Day with a bonfire complete with Herman(*sic*) Goering effigy. Proceeds of the celebration were sent to the Red Cross.

VJ Day celebrated. Rejoicing now that it's finally all over. 15 August 1945, saw the complete end of the war with the Japanese surrender. A street party in Howarth Road was all set to celebrate a day they would always remember.

Lancashire Daily Post.

No. 18,252 | REGISTERED AT THE GENERAL POST OFFICE AS A NEWSPAPER THURSDAY, AUGUST 16, 1945 Published Daily, 1½d.

HIROHITO ORDERS "CEASE FIRE"

THE MAN WHO THREATENED U.S. AIRMEN

Japan's new Premier, 57-year-old Prince Haruhiko Higashikuni, was quoted by Tokio radio in 1942 as saying that captured Allied airmen would be tried and might be sentenced to death.—Reuter.

FOREIGN OFFICE HOLIDAY WHILE U.S. NEGOTIATES

BY OUR DIPLOMATIC CORRESPONDENT

MR. BEVIN at the Foreign Office, and the permanent officials under him, are enjoying what is officially called "a well deserved rest." In other words: There is not much for our diplomats to do at this moment.

The reason is that the conduct of the negotiation with the Japanese has been left to the State Department in Washington. Mr. Attlee has described the American effort in the Pacific war as "prodigious," and has certified that without it Japanese resistance could have gone on for a very long time yet. The British, Russian and Chinese Governments, therefore, have agreed to leave the leading part in the negotiation with the Japanese Emperor to the Americans.

MACARTHUR'S ADVISER

Mr. Truman intends, I learn, to appoint Mr. Grew, ex-Ambassador to Tokio and at present Deputy Secretary of State, to be General MacArthur's political adviser in Japan. His place will be filled, Washington reports, by Assistant Under Secretary W. Clayton, who is at present in London discussing economic problems on which he is an expert.

The holiday at the Foreign Office will last until the first week in September, when a meeting is appointed in London of the British, American, Russian and Chinese Foreign Ministers or their deputies to discuss first of all the terms of the peace treaty with Italy.

UNCLE OF JAP EMPRESS IS NEW PREMIER

EMPEROR HIROHITO ordered the cease fire on all Japanese war fronts at 1 30 a.m. (B. S. T.) to-day, says Tokio radio.

The radio added that it might take some time for the order to reach isolated garrisons.

At the same time the agency reported the formation of a new Japanese Cabinet under 57-year-old Lieut.-General Prince Haruhiko Higashikuni, uncle of the Empress and Supreme Lord Counsellor since last April.

Lieut.-General Okamoto, Jap military attache in Rome, committed suicide at Zurich, to-day.

A message from General MacArthur had told the Japs to send representatives to the American H.Q. at Manila to receive instructions for carrying out the surrender terms. It added, "The representative will be accompanied by competent advisors representing the Japanese Army, Navy and Air Force."

General MacArthur said to-day that after the signal corps had been sending message No. 1 for several hours, with no acknowledgement, transmitting facilities in the U.S. were asked to assist.

By the early evening many agencies in the U.S. and in neutral capitals were bombarding the Japanese with these directives. By 9 p.m. an acknowledgement was received that the message had reached Tokio and had been understood.

The Japanese later stated that their surrender representatives will arrive at the island of Ie on their way to Manila between 2 a.m. and 7 a.m. (B.S.T.) Friday, according to a National Broadcasting Company broadcast from the Pacific.

LUZON HILLS COMBED

Allied psychological warfare loudspeaker trucks have begun combing the hills of Luzon calling on the Japanese to surrender honourably.

Australian troops have also begun sending messages to the trapped Japanese in the various islands.

In Manila, everyone is asking whether General Yamashita, Japan's military hero, who was cornered recently in the Carabello Mountains, will surrender or commit hara kiri.

Shanghai is to be the new Chinese H.Q. for Eastern China under the Chungking High Command's plan to take over former Japanese-held territory, said New Delhi radio to-day.

The newly appointed Mayor of Shanghai is on his way to take up his post.

—Reuter and B.U.P.

General MacArthur

Surrender Escort

An official broadcast from Okinawa, stating that a squadron of Lightning fighters would leave Okinawa at 9 p.m. (British Summer Time) to-night, with their rendezvous Sata Misaki, where the Japanese surrender 'plane is to leave Japan, has been heard in Guam.—B.U.P.

Red Army Still Fights On

FIGHTING continues in Manchuria, as far as is known to-day.

Marshal Vassilevsky's forces are pressing forward to close the

Australia Hits Out at Mikado

"FIRST SHOT IN

25 PER CENT. MORE PETROL

Officially announced this afternoon that the basic petrol ration for three-monthly period, September to November, is to be increased by the equivalent of 25 per cent. on present basic ration.

Increase will raise average monthly mileage obtainable from 120 miles to 150 miles a month. Basic ration for cars up to nine horse-power will be increased from 12 gallons for the three months, to 15 gallons; 10 to 13 horse-power from 15 to 18 gallons; 14 to 19 horse-power from 18 to 24 gallons; and 20 horse-power and over from 21 to 25 gallons.

Announcement adds that as and when additional supplies become available, present petrol restrictions will be relaxed with view to the speedy withdrawal of rationing when circumstances permit.

RELEASE SPEED-UP PLANS FOR M.E. TROOPS

ROME, Thursday.

BRITISH troops in the Mediterranean theatre can now expect a speed-up in release or re-deployment plans.

Officials told a Reuter correspondent that present plans are working smoothly and well up to schedule, but they could give no definite date by which the effect of the speed-up would become noticeable.

Although the American military authorities announced, a month ago, that the U.S. army of occupation, in Italy, would total some 28,000 men, British Army officials still decline to make any statement on the numbers of British troops who will join the Americans in the

MR. CHURCHILL'S VIEW OF ATOMIC BOMB

Secret Should Not Be Passed On

SPEAKING in the Commons, to-day, Mr. Churchill, referring to the end of the war, said in the first days of the Potsdam Conference, President Truman and he approved a plan submitted by the Combined Chiefs of Staff for great battles and landings in Malaya, the Netherlands East Indies, and in the homeland of Japan itself.

These operations involved an effort not surpassed, and no one can measure the cost in British and American life and treasure which they would have required.

Speaking of the atomic bomb, Mr. Churchill said, "Success beyond all dreams crowned this sombre, magnificent venture of our American allies."

Before the bomb was used repeated warnings were emphasised by heavy bombing attacks to secure the exodus of populations from the threatened towns.

ATOMIC BOMB

He could not associate himself with those who said that the bomb ought not to have been used at all.

If the Germans and Japanese had discovered it they would

M.P.S' ATOMIC BOMB QUERIES

A BARRAGE of 211 questions to the Ministers of the new Government will open at to-morrow's sitting of the House of Commons. They range from the atomic bomb to the shortage of washing soda in the suburbs, from the size of secondary school classes to the future of the cotton industry.

Queues, requisitioned houses, herring fishing and the petrol ration are other problems on which guidance is sought.

On Tuesday the Prime Minister will be asked whether the Government will take the initiative, in consultation with U.S.A., the Soviet Union, France, and China in "calling an international conference to discuss methods of ensuring effective international control of atomic power and of the materials and processes associated with its production and use."

MR. SILVERMAN'S QUESTION

Mr. Sydney Silverman (Lab.,

NO ZONES IN JAPAN

President Truman says occupation of Japan will not be split up into zones, but probably shared by troops of Big Four Allies under command of MacArthur.—Reuter

The Japanese are beaten!

Wartime Prime Minister Winston Churchill speaks to the crowds in the Market Square from the Harris building steps during the 1945 General Election. His son, Randolph (left) was one of two Conservative candidates for Preston. Both candidates were defeated in a Labour landslide victory.

This was the crowd that gathered on the Market Square to see and hear Winston Churchill speak. The rectangular building on the square is a public air-raid shelter.

Sweet rationing ends! These Preston youngsters couldn't believe it on 25 April 1949, that sweet rationing was really over at long last.

Yes, we have some bananas today! Bananas didn't reappear on sale in Preston until June 1950 – five years after the war in Europe had ended. These youngsters are not too sure whether or not they like this strange yellow fruit.

The Deepdale greats – The Invincibles is a name still remembered when the days of Preston North End's FA Cup and Football League championship winning team of 1888-89 are recalled. Back row: (left to right): G.Drummond, R.H.Howarth, Mr R.J.Hanbury MP, Mr W.E.Tomlinson MP, D.Russell, R.Holmes, Major W.Sudell (chairman), J.Graham, Dr R.H.Mill-Roberts. Seated: J.Gordon, J.Ross, J.Goodall, F.Dewhurst and S.Thomson.

A disastrous fire in March 1933, destroyed Preston North End's 30-year-old Town End Stand. The fire was started by a cigarette end igniting waste paper which had gathered under the stand – shades of the later Valley Parade cause! Luckily, the Deepdale ground was empty at the time. This view is of the front of the stadium. The metal pillars were bent by the intense heat.

Return to the top. Preston North End won promotion to Division One in 1934 after being in Division Two for nine years. Here Bill Tremelling, the captain, is being congratulated and the team introduced to the Mayor and Mayoress of Preston. Bill Scott, the trainer, is on the extreme right and Jimmy Milne (later manager) on the extreme left.

Preston North End players lacing up for practice on Dick, Kerrs ground (now Ashton Park) at the start of the 1936-37 season. Front (left to right): Holdcroft, Beresford, Burns. Back: L.Gallimore, Lowe, F.Gallimore and Bill Shankly.

Five of the Preston North End forwards in training for the 1937 FA Cup Final team which lost 3-1 to Sunderland. The following year North End beat Huddersfield 1-0 in the Cup Final. From left: F. O'Donnell, Beresford, Fagan, Dougall, H. O'Donnell.

Wembley victory. Preston North End captain, Tom Smith, borne shoulder high, holds the FA Cup at Wembley in 1938 after Preston beat Huddersfield Town 1-0 with a last-minute penalty. Included are Bill Shankly, Andy Beattie, Frank Gallimore with glimpses of goalkeeper Holdcroft and match-winner George Mutch (rear).

Apart from the 1939 car models, this scene of Preston North End's West Stand has not changed much. Loxham's Garages Limited no longer exists and neither will this view of the West Stand when the present plans to rebuild it materialise around 1996.

A young genius unrecognised. The small boy stood on the engine buffer (centre) in short trousers is 13-year-old Tom Finney, the reserve player with Preston Schoolboys' team in 1936 when they travelled to meet West Ham Boys in the English School's Trophy Final in London. Tom was considered too small to be selected. The match was a draw and the teams shared the trophy.

Tom Finney and his charming bride, Elsie, in 1945 outside Emmanuel Church after their wedding.

Bill Dean, FA Colts trainer, massages Tom Finney's leg before a game at Blackpool watched by George Bromilow (Southport) and Colin Henderson (Heysham), the two linesmen, and Ken Horton (Preston North End).

Tom's farewell – Tom Finney accepts the crowd's applause prior to the kick-off in his final appearance for Preston North End at Deepdale in April 1960, when they beat Luton Town 2-0.

Tom Finney, club president, removes the first turf at Deepdale in 1986 prior to the laying of the controversial plastic pitch which was removed eight years later.

Preston's Famous Ladies. Over the years there have been several Dick, Kerr's Ladies Football teams. Here is the original team which was started in 1917 by women workers at the Preston factory. They began playing to raise money for the Moor Park military hospital during World War One and went on to win world fame for years afterwards.

A group of schoolboy admirers watch Dick, Kerr's Ladies team practice on Moor Park in 1937.

Preston's famous Dick, Kerr's Ladies line up against Weymouth Ladies in 1946.

Joan Whalley (holding the ball) discusses tactics with other members of the Dick, Kerr's Ladies Team in the 1946 era.

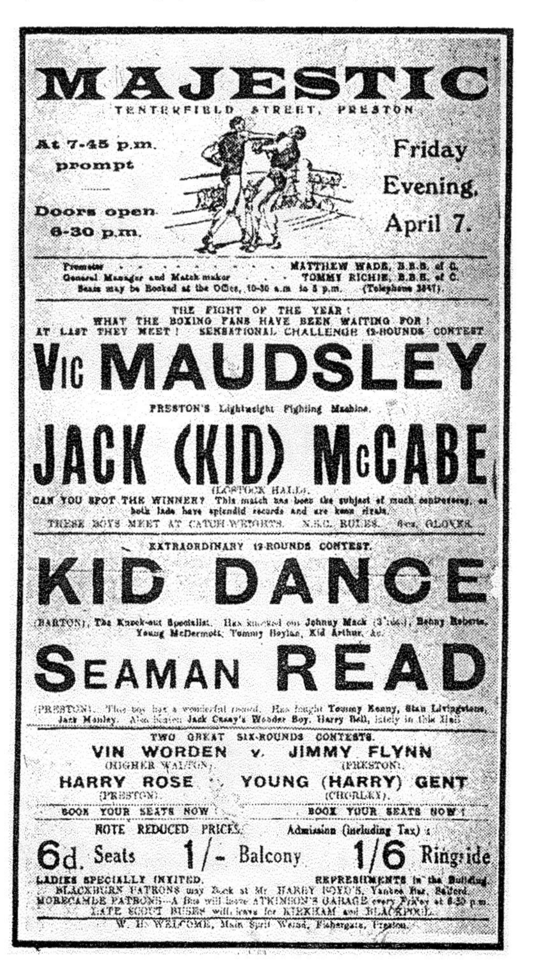

Far left: The Majestic in Tenterfield Street, Preston, owned by market trader Matt Wade, was used for boxing, wrestling, roller-skating and dancing. Most of the boxers on this 1937 bill were local fighters.

Left: Johnny Sullivan, the Preston middleweight, in 1954 when he was the British and Empire champion and a Lonsdale Belt holder.

Johnny Sullivan, in the open-top car, is given a VIP reception in Preston after winning his 1954 championship fight at Harringay.

Around the same time that Johnny Sullivan was in the entertainment spotlight, so also was Preston's world famous golden trumpeter Eddie Calvert. Eddie first started playing with a Preston band and went on to appear at the London Palladium and around the world. He won the Golden Disc, awarded for the highest number of records sold.

Wonder walker Tom Benson pictured during his long distance walk in 1986 around Moor Park, Preston. Tom set up seven world walking records between 1976 and 1986 including his 415-mile pounding, non-stop, around the park. A new Preston road, Tom Benson Way, was named after him.

Royal Visits

The royals who came to Preston – and gave it the go by!
Queen Victoria passed through Preston Railway Station many times on her way to and from Balmoral on the royal train, yet never once stopped to visit the town. On many occasions her carriage window curtains were drawn when passing through Preston Station.

The ill-fated Russian Tsar Nicholas II and his family did at least get off their royal train in 1896 when passing through Preston from Balmoral. They dined in a special dining-room on what is now platforms 3 and 4. They exercised their dogs along the platform after breakfasting. No one was allowed on the station, not even the Mayor of Preston who wanted to officially greet them.

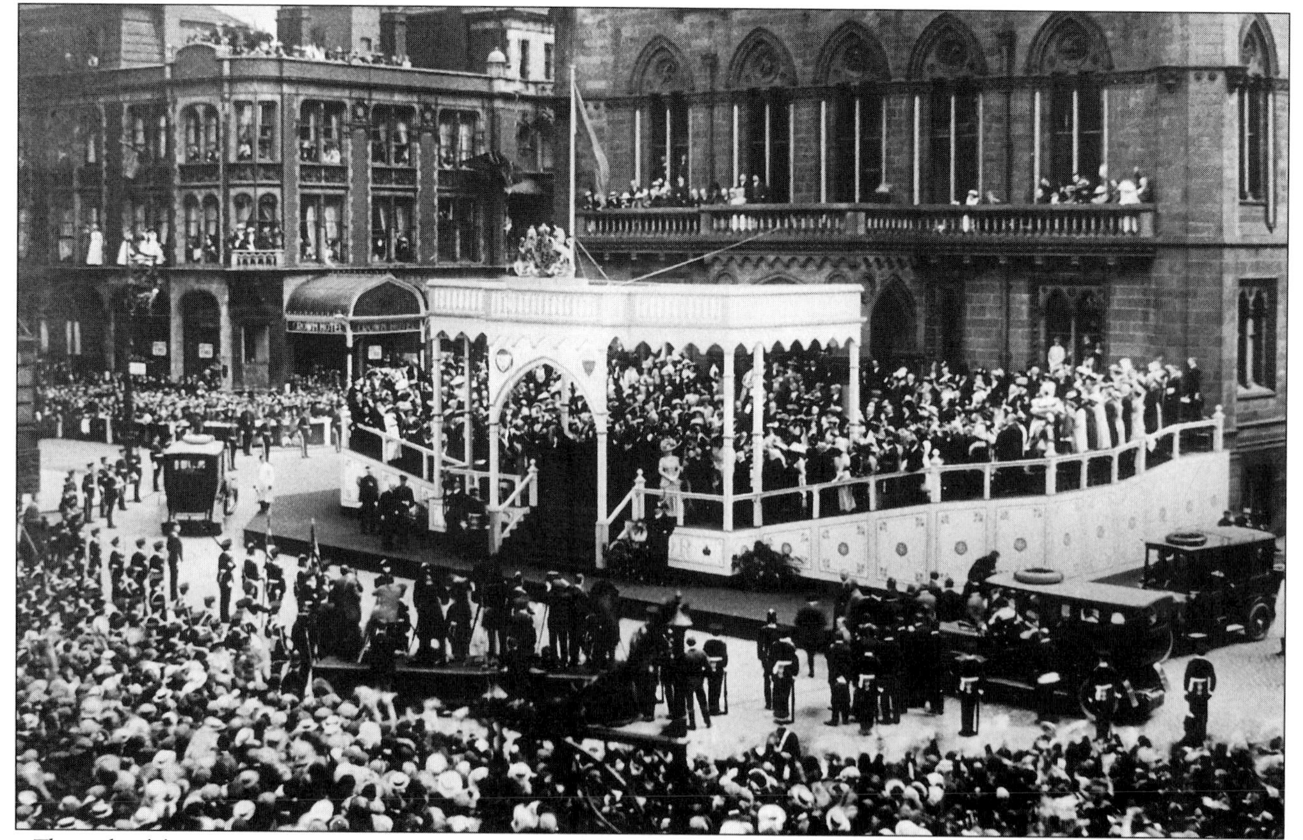

The only visit to Preston ever made by King George V and Queen Mary was in 1913. Here they are at the old Town Hall greeting the crowds. Their visit included a tour of Horrocks' cotton mill.

A friendly royal wave on the old Town Hall steps from future Queen, Princess Elizabeth and her husband the Duke of Edinburgh at the start of their 1949 visit to Preston. The Mayor, Alderman R.Ainsworth, is on the left.

Royalty are not often photographed while dining. The Princess in 1949 is seen here at County Hall, Preston, during her visit with Prince Philip, the Duke of Edinburgh.

Queen Elizabeth (now Queen Mother) waves from the old Town Hall steps. On her right is Princess Margaret and on the Queen's left is King George VI. Flanking the royal trio are the Mayor and Mayoress, Alderman and Mrs M.Williamson. This 1951 visit was to inspect the King's Duchy of Lancaster estate in Wyresdale.

The crowds dispersing in North Road in 1951 after the royal car had passed northwards. The small shops (right) are now warehouses and a service station. On the left are now maisonettes. The peak-roof building in the distance is the Picturedrome cinema, Brackenbury Place.

Prince Philip and Queen Elizabeth being greeted by the Mayor of Preston, Councillor Joe Hood, on their arrival at the Town Hall in 1977. The royal couple were visiting Lancashire to mark the Queen's Silver Jubilee as monarch.

Her moment of glory. This little girl is shy and overwhelmed after being presented to the Queen during the 1977 Silver Jubilee visit to Preston Town Hall, escorted by the Mayor.

All is revealed. Two years later the Queen was back in Preston to unveil the ancient obelisk which was restored to the Market Square in 1979. One royal tug and off come the wraps!

Admirer Elizabeth Barron presents a posy to the Queen after Her Majesty had unveiled the obelisk.

All smiles for the Queen as she steps out of the Town Hall on her 1979 walkabout.

At the Harris Museum and Art building the Queen signs a portrait of herself. At her side is the Mayor, Councillor Arthur Taylor.

A serious-looking Queen admires the Preston Corporation civic regalia in the Harris Museum.

Smiles again for the crowd as the Queen leaves the Harris Building with Town Clerk Mr Harry Heap and the Mayor, Councillor Harry Taylor.

Even the rain can't wash away a royal smile for these ex-service veterans during the Queen's 1979 visit to Fulwood Barracks.

In 1980 the Queen again visited Preston as part of her tour of the Duchy of Lancaster estates. Here she is greeted by the Mayor, Councillor Dennis Kehoe.

Princess Alexandra unveils the commemorative plaque in Arkwright House in 1980 after it had been restored. The house is in Stoneygate.

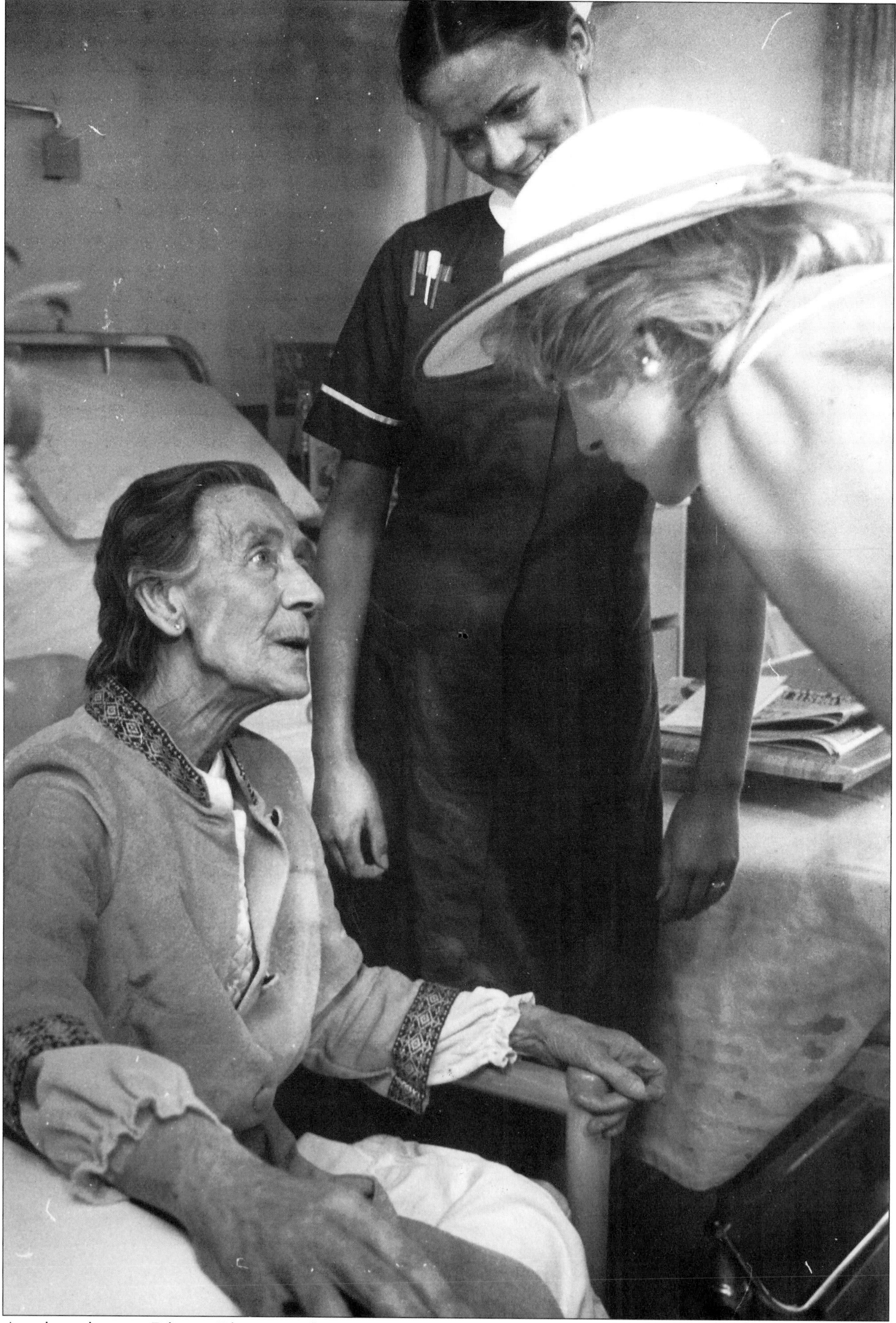

A caring princess – Princess Diana stops for a sympathetic word with a sick patient in the Royal Preston Hospital after the 1983 opening.

Hi there, Highness! How about chatting with me down here? Princess Diana in the Children's Ward after she officially opened the Royal Preston Hospital in 1983.

Healing the Sick

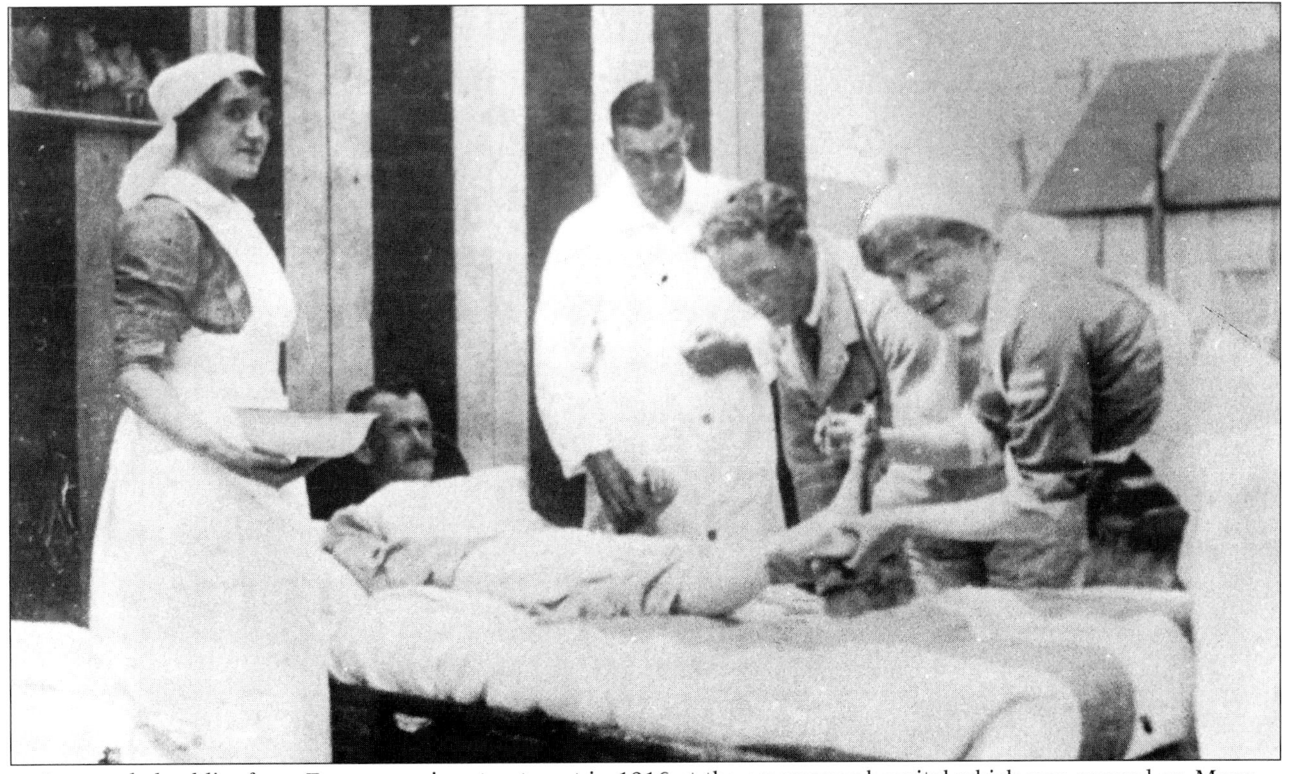

A wounded soldier from France receives treatment in 1916 at the emergency hospital which was opened on Moor Park, Preston.

A skeleton out of the cupboard! This grisly photograph merely shows one of the nurses' training classrooms in use in the Thirties at Preston Royal Infirmary.

This X-ray machine was the latest technology for treating cancer at Preston Royal Infirmary in 1933.

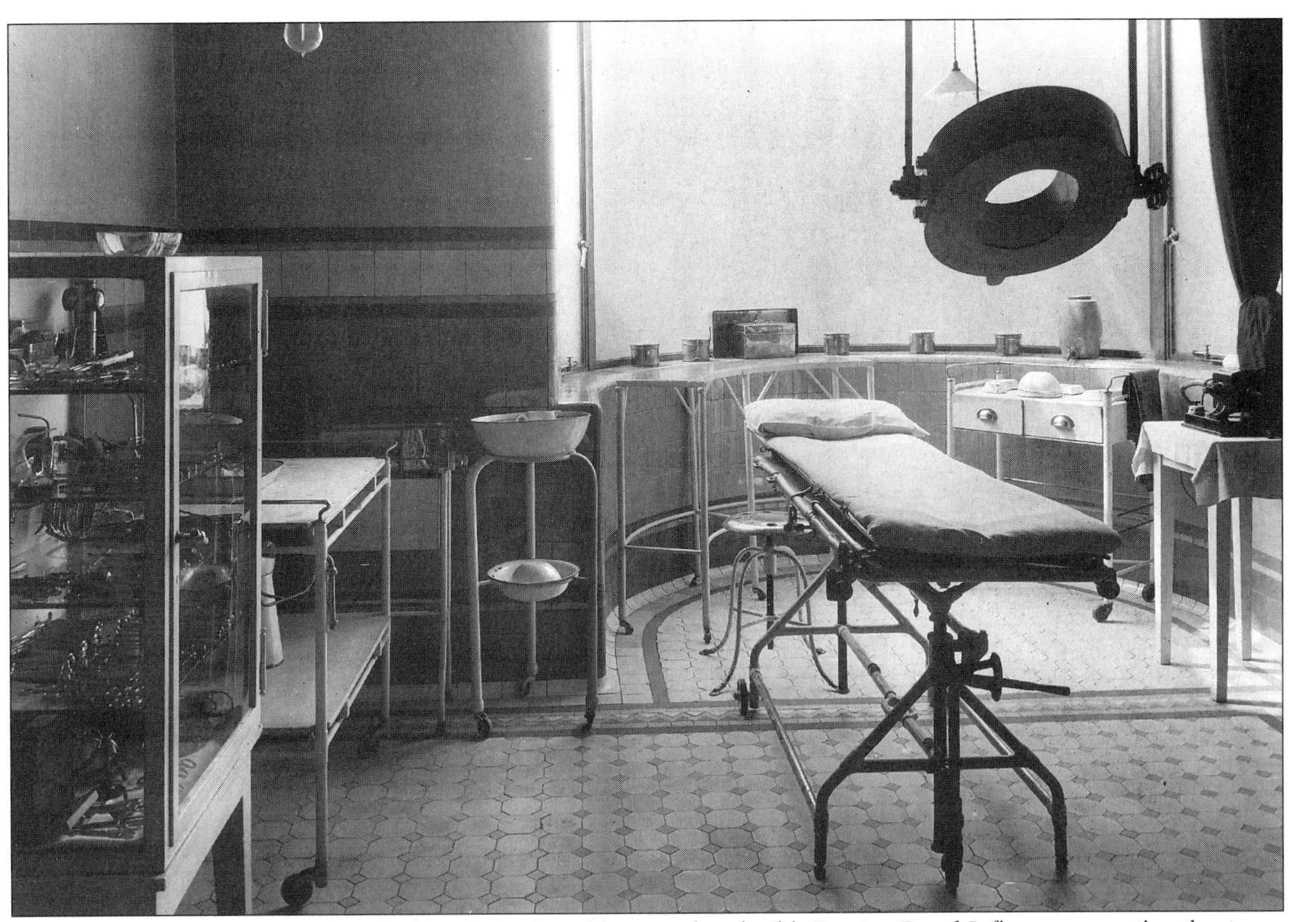

Fluorescent lighting was unheard of in 1936 when this was taken in this Preston Royal Infirmary operating theatre.

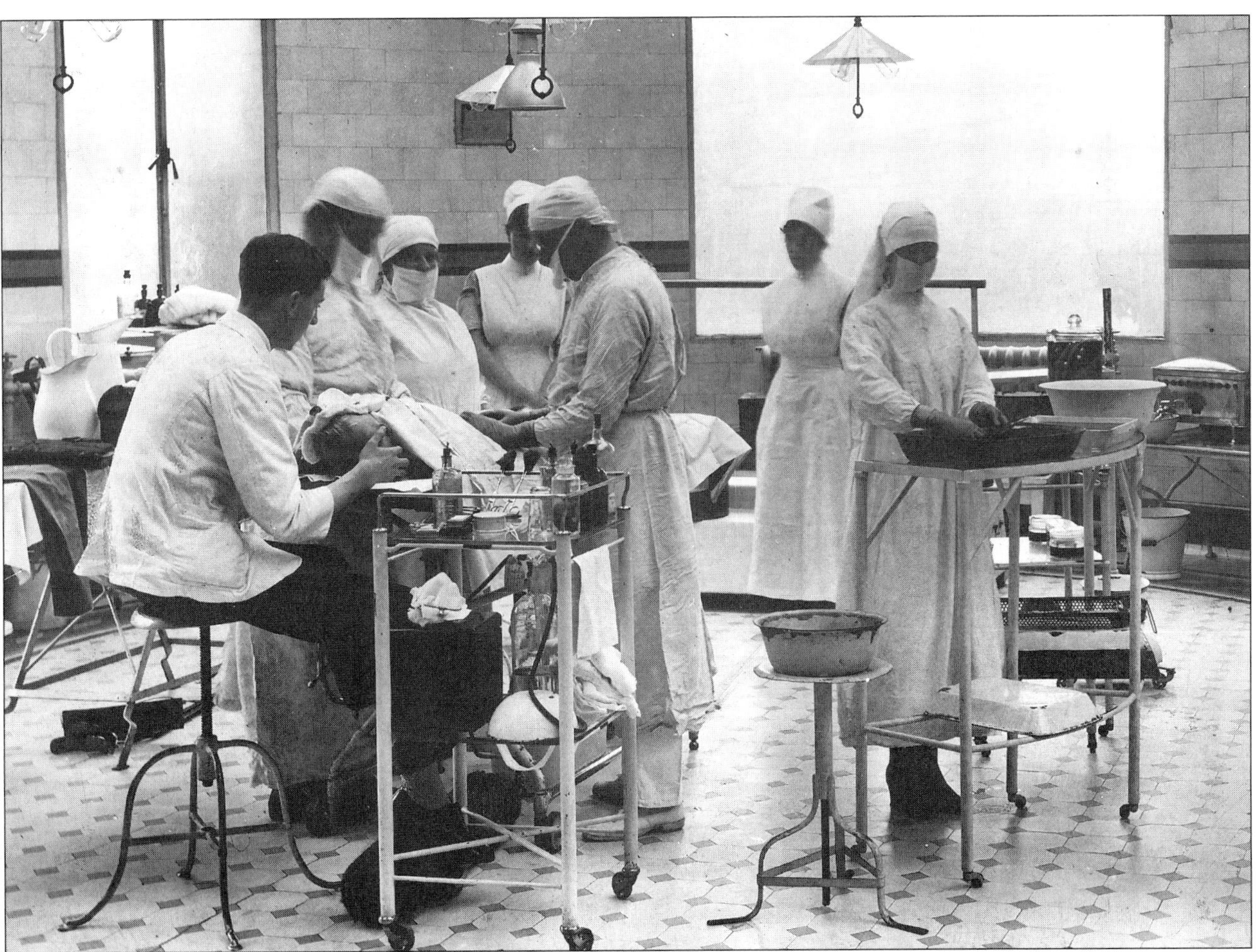

And this was how they performed operations in Preston Royal Infirmary.

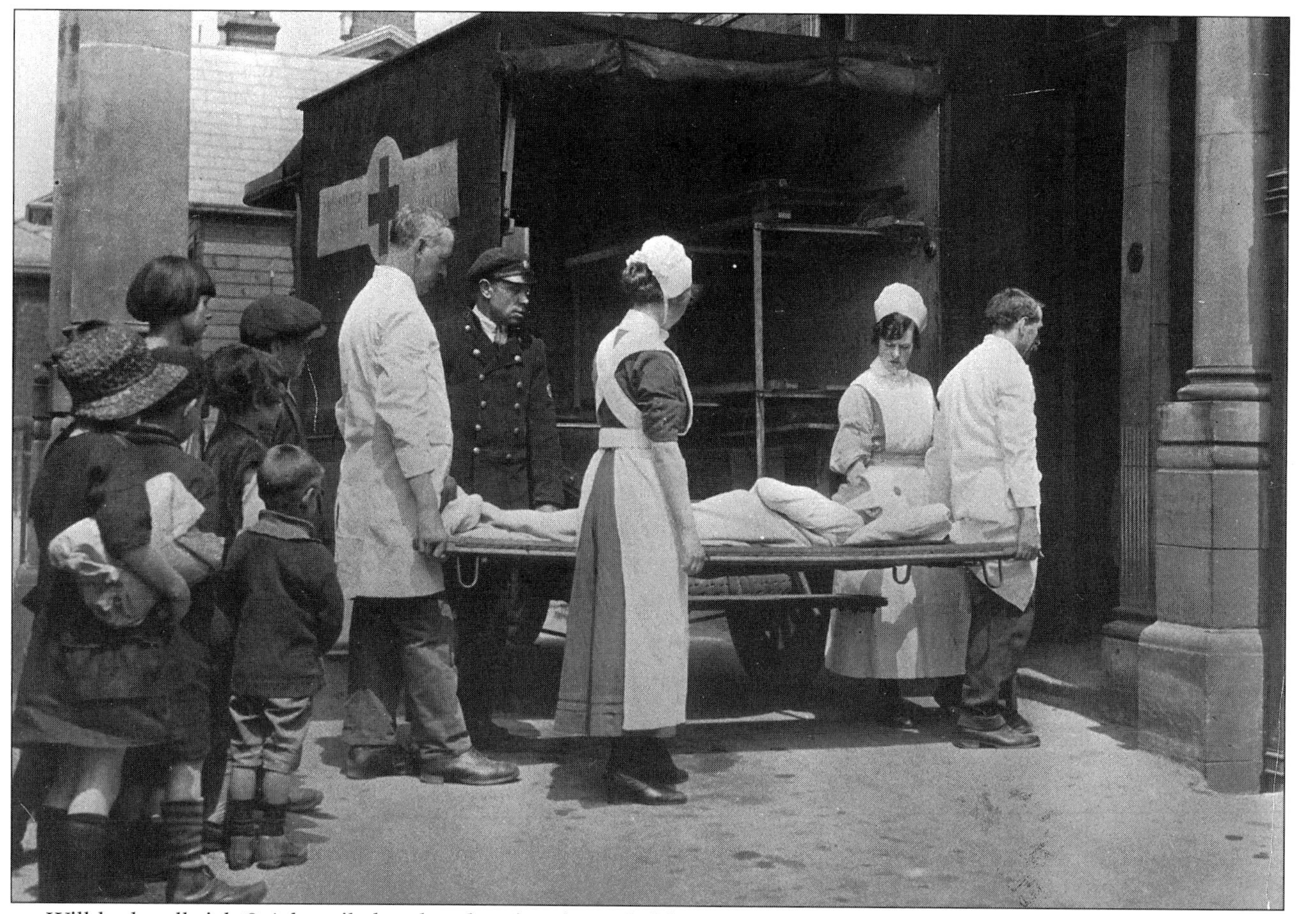

Will he be all right? A heavily bandaged patient is carried into Preston Royal Infirmary in the 1920s, watched by young and sympathetic onlookers. Note the canvas-rolled ambulance exit door.

There was no NHS in existence in 1935 when these out-patients awaited their turn at Preston Royal Infirmary. Casualties were brought into the infirmary by the same entrance and the smell of antiseptics and chloroform was always present.

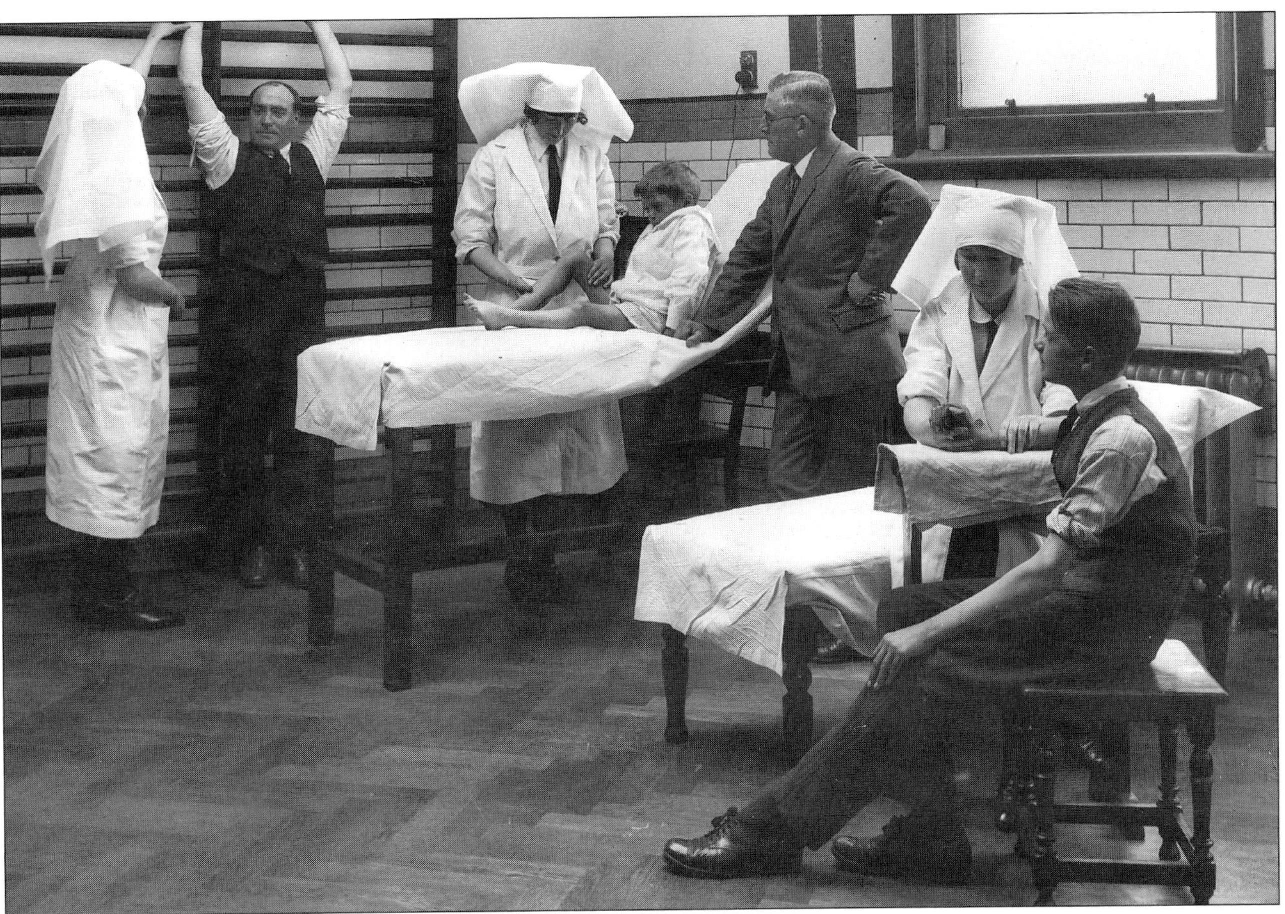

Preston Royal Infirmary patients receiving massage and medical treatment in 1936.

The new maternity wing which was opened at Preston Royal Infirmary in 1936 by the Countess of Derby. The money was raised mainly by voluntary subscriptions.

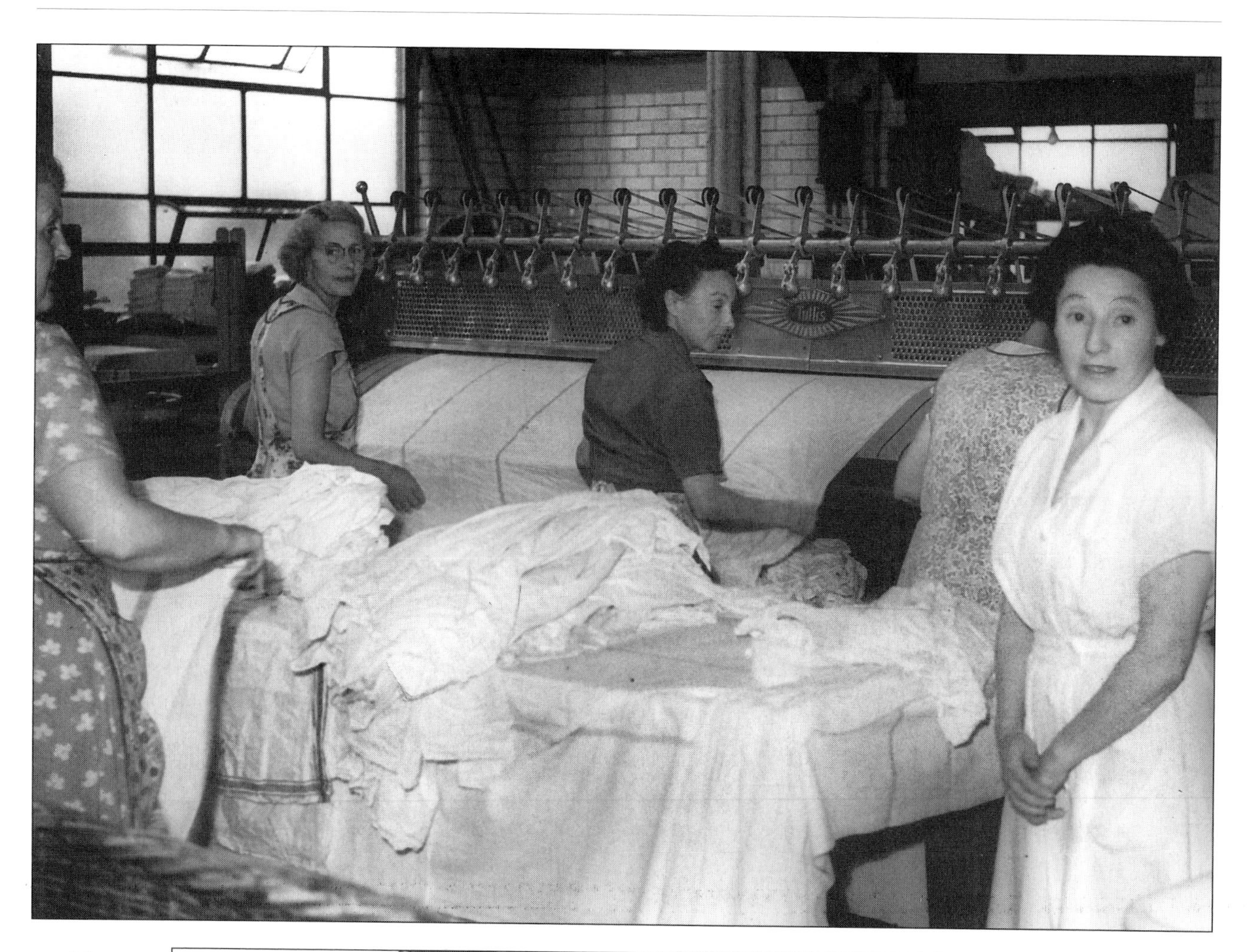

The Infirmary laundry machine dealt with 29,000 pieces of washing every week in 1960.

Preston Royal Infirmary entrance, Stanleyfield Road, in 1960.

By 1973 it had been changed to this.

By the time Preston Royal Infirmary was phased out in the 1980s it had become a hotchpotch of temporary added buildings such as this one.

St Joseph's Hospital, Mount Street, began as a sick-poor hospital in 1877 and was run by an order of nuns. Around 1935 the hospital was extended. Here it is being blessed by the Bishop of Lancaster, the Rt Revd T.W.Pearson OSB, on the extreme right is Preston MP Adrian Moreing. The hospital closed in 1987.

The year 1966 saw Sharoe Green Hospital's new section in course of erection. The original part was once the workhouse hospital.

Fulwood Continuation Hospital on Longsands Lane just before it closed in 1984. Now it is part of a housing estate.

Rain and Shine

The winter of 1929 proved an Arctic affair when the Ribble froze over. This is a downstream view of the old Penwortham bridge.

Workmen casting piles to safeguard the Boulevard, Frenchwood, after severe flooding in 1927.

When Preston Borough had its own fire brigade it was its generous practice to pump water from the Ribble into Happy Valley, Avenham Park, during frosty spells so that townsfolk could skate and slide. Here they are in 1933 doing just that.

And here is the result, ice that is safe for all to venture on.

The first winter of World War Two was long remembered for its severity. This photograph was taken on 31 January, 1940. It shows the frozen River Ribble near the Continental Hotel.

Tragedy – the scarred bank of the River Ribble at Red Scar where an avalanche of sand, clay and stones suddenly buried two anglers in 1950 after heavy rains. The anglers were never seen again.

A high-tide view of the Ribble Valley at Walton-le-Dale in the December flood of 1951.

Dense fog in wintertime could make life unhealthy and miserable. This was the scene in December 1957 at the Maudland railway sidings, when a train became derailed.

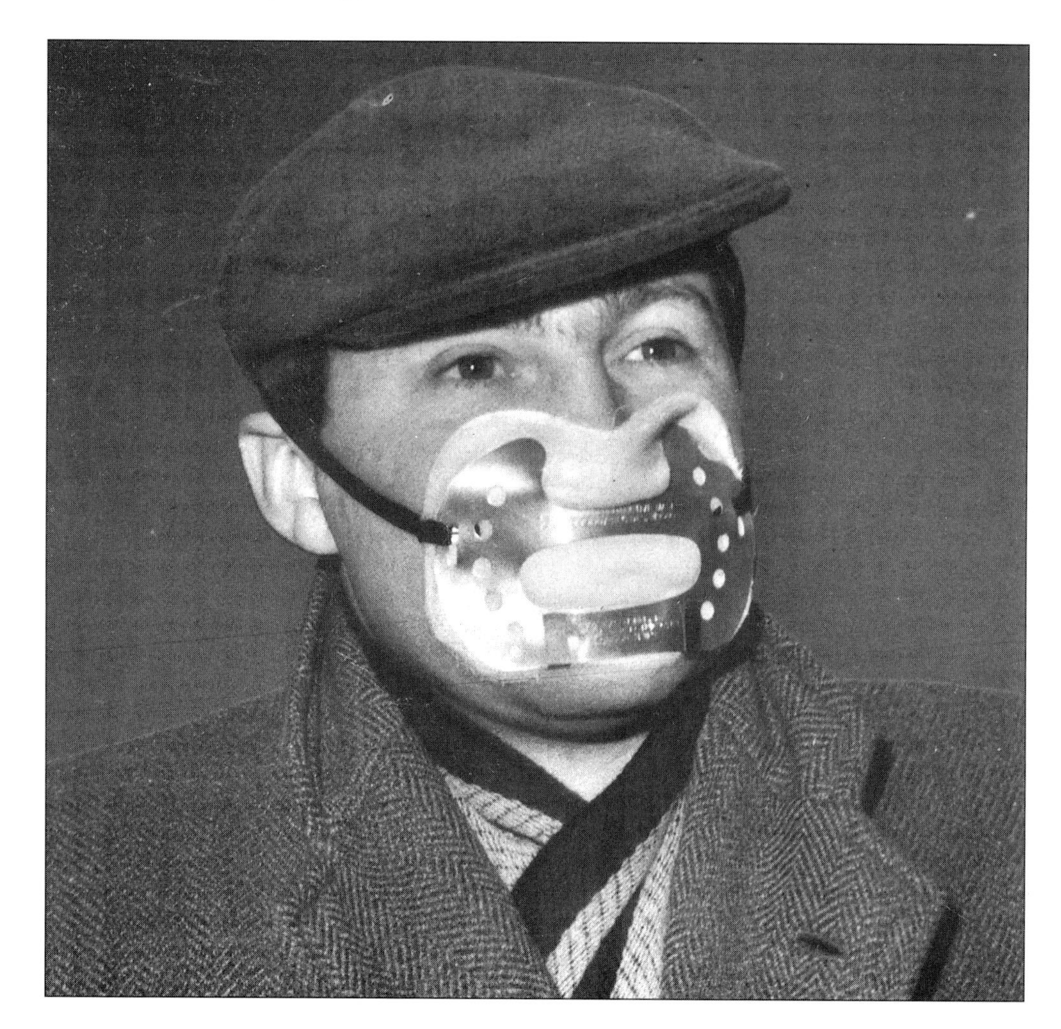

No, he isn't a masked robber. It was just one way of trying to beat the winter smog that used to be common in industrial towns. This smog mask was on sale in a Fishergate chemists in 1959 after doctors had advised the public to take precautions.

The River Ribble floods meeting the tides can cause anxious moments in the Broadgate and Lower Penwortham areas. Sandbags have been placed where the river wall was washed away in 1980.

No entry – except for boats! Another flooded area in October 1980, was Mill Lane, Fulwood, where Cadley Brook overflowed.

Two inches of rain fell when this was taken in 1980 on the A6 at Brock near the Green Man Inn. It was the wettest October for 12 years in Lancashire.

One of the hottest summers in the North-West occurred when this photograph was taken in 1983. Temperatures soared into the 90s and these girls chose Avenham Park ornamental lake into which to cool off. The following summer, 1984, was also a scorcher.

Subscribers

Barry Ashton
Paul H Bannister
Stuart Robert Black
Kevin & Jennifer Brennan
Stephen Briscoe
Winifred Olive Britton
Brian, Carole, Laurence & Edward Brown
Olive B Buckland
Margaret Cartwright
Mr R D Challen
Judith Charnley
Harry & Marie Charnock (Australia)
Mrs & Mrs F A Childs
Barbara Crabtree
Ian John Crabtree
Peter J Croft
Lorraine Cruickshank
Robert Alan Driver
Kathleen Eaton
Mr Jimmy Farrington
Mr John Paul Fitzsimmons
James & Margaret Fletcher
Vincent Ford
J B Frankland
Susan M Greenall
Andrew Robert Gutteridge
Mary & Bernard Halpin
John Hamer
Mr & Mrs W O Hearn & Family (Sparks, Nevada, USA)
Joan & Norman Hindle
Robert Helvin
M P Hopkinson
Mr R H Jewell
Arthur Jones
Derek Jones
Peter B Kenyon
K H King
Mrs Christine Anne Kitching
Joe Latham
Martin McDonagh
Robert McWilliam
Brenda Maher
William Stanley Marsden
Thomas F Marsh

Mr Harold Martindale
Alf P P Morris
Kathrine & David Muir
Ian, Stephanie, Clare & Benjamin Murray
Mr R Audrey Musson
Mrs B S Newton
Joe & Elsie Newton
Dave & Sheila Odlum
Elizabeth O'Reilly
Mr Raymond Panzer
F E Parkinson
Jack Parkinson
Wiliam B Pearson
Rita & Bernard Raby
A H Richardson
Mr G Riding
Douglas Seed
Francis Albert Sherlow
Lucas Simon-Sergeant
David R Simpson
Gordon Small
Harry & Margaret Smith & Family (Fulwood)
Darren Samuel Spencer
Mrs Margaret Stephens
Joyce & Gerry Stokes
Mr Alan Stones
Mr & Mrs F W Swanton
Mr E Swarbrick
Mr Michael Paul Sweetmore
Jean & Frank Taylor
Mr & Mrs F D True
Aidan Turner-Bishop
John Unsworth
Neil F Walker
Dreenie & Cyril Wareing
Caroline Welton
Peter & Margaret Welton
Mrs Sandra Whalley
Mrs B Whittle
Sofia Whittle
Susan Wiggans
Alan Wilding (Wing Commander, RAF, Ret)
Nancy Wilkes
John Wilkinson
Robert Wright